KT-219-977

Quentin Skinner

MACHIAVELLI

A Very Short Introduction

OXFORD
UNIVERSITY PRESS

OXFORD
UNIVERSITY PRESS

Great Clarendon Street, Oxford OX2 6DP

Oxford University Press is a department of the University of Oxford.
It furthers the University's objective of excellence in research, scholarship,
and education by publishing worldwide in

Oxford New York

Auckland Bangkok Buenos Aires Cape Town Chennai
Dar es Salaam Delhi Hong Kong Istanbul Karachi Kolkata
Kuala Lumpur Madrid Melbourne Mexico City Mumbai Nairobi
São Paulo Shanghai Taipei Tokyo Toronto

Oxford is a registered trade mark of Oxford University Press
in the UK and in certain other countries

Published in the United States
by Oxford University Press Inc., New York

First published 1981 as an Oxford University Press paperback
Reissued 1996
First published as a Very Short Introduction 2000

British Library Cataloguing in Publication Data
Data available

Library of Congress Cataloging in Publication Data
Data available

ISBN 978-0-19-285407-0

21

Typeset by RefineCatch Ltd, Bungay, Suffolk
Printed in Great Britain by
Ashford Colour Press Ltd, Gosport, Hampshire

Contents

27174

List of Illustrations

27174

The publisher and the author apologize for any errors or omissions in
the above list. If contacted they will be pleased to rectify these at the
earliest opportunity.

Preface

An earlier version of this introduction was published in the Past Masters series in 1981. I remain greatly indebted to Keith Thomas for inviting me to contribute to his series, to the staff of the Oxford University Press (especially Henry Hardy) for much editorial help at that time, and to John Dunn, Susan James, J. G. A. Pocock, and Keith Thomas for reading my original manuscript with meticulous care and providing me with many valuable comments. For expert help with the preparation of this new edition I am again very grateful to the editorial staff at the Press, and especially to Shelley Cox for much patience and encouragement.

For this new edition I have thoroughly revised my text and brought the bibliography up to date, but I have not altered my basic line of argument. I still think of Machiavelli essentially as the exponent of a neo-classical form of humanist political thought. I argue in addition that the most original and creative aspects of his political vision are best understood as a series of polemical – sometimes even satirical – reactions against the humanist assumptions he inherited and basically continued to endorse. While my principal aim has been to provide a straightforward introduction to Machiavelli's views on statecraft, I hope that this interpretation may also be of some interest to specialists in the field.

When quoting from Boethius, Cicero, Livy, Sallust, and Seneca, I have used the translations published in the Loeb classical library. When I cite from Machiavelli's *Correspondence*, *Legations*, and so-called *Caprices* (*Ghiribizzi*) the translations are my own. When quoting from *The Prince* I have used the translation by Russell Price in Machiavelli, *The Prince* ed. Quentin Skinner and Russell Price (Cambridge, 1988). When quoting from Machiavelli's other works I have relied (with kind permission) on the excellent English versions in Allan Gilbert, trans.: *Machiavelli: The Chief Works and Others* (3 vols, Duke University Press, 1965). When I cite from the *Correspondence* and the *Legations*, I identify the source by placing a 'C' or an 'L' in brackets, as appropriate, together with the page-reference after each quotation. When I refer to other works by Machiavelli, I make it contextually clear in each case which text I am citing, and simply add the page-references in brackets. Full details of all the editions I am using can be found in the list of 'Works by Machiavelli Quoted in the Text' on p. 101.

I need to make two further points about translations. I have ventured in a few places to amend Gilbert's renderings in order to keep closer to Machiavelli's exact phraseology. And I have held to my belief that Machiavelli's pivotal concept of *virtú* (*virtus* in Latin) cannot be translated into modern English by any single word or manageable series of periphrases. I have consequently left these terms in their original form throughout. This is not to say, however, that I fail to discuss their meanings; on the contrary, much of my text can be read as an explication of what I take Machiavelli to have meant by them.

Introduction

Machiavelli died nearly 500 years ago, but his name lives on as a byword for cunning, duplicity, and the exercise of bad faith in political affairs. 'The murderous Machiavel', as Shakespeare called him, has never ceased to be an object of hatred to moralists of all persuasions, conservatives and revolutionaries alike. Edmund Burke claimed to see 'the odious maxims of a machiavellian policy' underlying the 'democratic tyranny' of the French Revolution. Marx and Engels attacked the principles of machiavellianism with no less vehemence, while insisting that the true exponents of 'machiavellian policy' are those who attempt 'to paralyse democratic energies' at periods of revolutionary change. The point on which both sides agree is that the evils of machiavellianism constitute one of the most dangerous threats to the moral basis of political life.

So much notoriety has gathered around Machiavelli's name that the charge of being a machiavellian still remains a serious accusation in political debate. When Henry Kissinger, for example, expounded his philosophy in a famous interview published in *The New Republic* in 1972, his interviewer remarked, after hearing him discuss his role as a presidential adviser, that 'listening to you, one sometimes wonders not how much you have influenced the President of the United States but to what extent you have been influenced by Machiavelli'. The suggestion was one that Kissinger showed himself extremely anxious to repudiate. Was he a machiavellian?' 'No, not at all.' Was he not influenced by Machiavelli to some degree?' 'To none whatever.'

What lies behind the sinister reputation Machiavelli has acquired? Is it really deserved? What views about politics and political morality does he actually put forward in his major works? These are the questions I hope to answer in the course of this book. I shall argue that, in order to understand Machiavelli's doctrines, we need to begin by recovering the problems he evidently saw himself confronting in *The Prince*, the *Discourses*, and his other works of political thought. To attain this perspective, we need in turn to reconstruct the context in which these works were originally composed – the intellectual context of classical and Renaissance philosophy, as well as the political context of Italian city-state life at the start of the sixteenth century. Once we restore Machiavelli to the world in which his ideas were initially formed, we can begin to appreciate the extraordinary originality of his attack on the prevailing moral assumptions of his age. And once we grasp the implications of his own moral outlook, we can readily see why his name is still so often invoked whenever the issues of political power and leadership are discussed.

Chapter 1
The Diplomat

The Humanist Background

Niccolò Machiavelli was born in Florence on 3 May 1469. We first hear of him playing an active part in the affairs of his native city in 1498, the year in which the regime controlled by Savonarola fell from power. Girolamo Savonarola, the Dominican prior of San Marco, whose prophetic sermons had dominated Florentine politics for the previous four years, was arrested for heresy early in April; soon afterwards the city's ruling council began to dismiss his remaining supporters from their positions in the government. One of those who lost his job as a result was Alessandro Braccesi, the head of the second chancery. At first the post was left unoccupied, but after a delay of several weeks the almost unknown name of Machiavelli was put forward as a possible replacement. He was barely 29 years old, and appears to have had no previous administrative experience. Yet his nomination went through without evident difficulty, and on 19 June he was duly confirmed by the great council as second chancellor of the Florentine republic.

By the time Machiavelli entered the chancery, there was a well-established method of recruitment to its major offices. In addition to giving evidence of diplomatic skills, aspiring officials were expected to display a high degree of competence in the so-called humane

1. The Palazzo Vecchio, Florence, where Machiavelli worked in the second chancery from 1498 until 1512.

disciplines. This concept of the *studia humanitatis* had been derived from Roman sources, and especially from Cicero, whose pedagogic ideals were revived by the Italian humanists of the fourteenth century and came to exercise a powerful influence on the universities and on the conduct of Italian public life. The humanists were distinguished first of all by their commitment to a particular theory about the proper contents of a 'truly humane' education. They expected their students to begin with the mastery of Latin, move on to the practice of rhetoric and the imitation of the finest classical stylists, and complete their studies with a close reading of ancient history and moral philosophy. They also popularized the long-standing belief that this type of training offers the best preparation for political life. As Cicero had repeatedly maintained, these disciplines nurture the values we principally need to acquire in order to serve our country well: a willingness to subordinate our private interests to the public good; a desire to fight against corruption and tyranny; and an ambition to reach out for the noblest goals of all, those of honour and glory for our country as well as for ourselves.

As the Florentines became increasingly imbued with these beliefs, they began to call on their leading humanists to fill the most prestigious positions in the city government. The practice may be said to have started with the appointment of Coluccio Salutati as chancellor in 1375, and it rapidly became the rule. While Machiavelli was growing up, the first chancellorship was held by Bartolomeo Scala, who retained his professorship at the university throughout his public career and continued to write on typically humanist themes, his main works being a moral treatise and a *History of the Florentines*. During Machiavelli's own time in the chancery, the same traditions were impressively upheld by Scala's successor, Marcello Adriani. He too transferred to the first chancellorship from a chair at the university, and he too continued to publish works of humanist scholarship, including a textbook on the teaching of Latin and a vernacular treatise *On the Education of the Florentine Nobility*.

The prevalence of these ideals helps to explain how Machiavelli came to be appointed at a relatively early age to a position of considerable responsibility in the administration of the republic. For his family, though neither rich nor highly aristocratic, was closely connected with some of the city's most exalted humanist circles. Machiavelli's father, Bernardo, who earned his living as a lawyer, was an enthusiastic student of the humanities. He was on close terms with several distinguished scholars, including Bartolomeo Scala, whose tract of 1483 *On Laws and Legal Judgements* took the form of a dialogue between himself and 'my friend and intimate', Bernardo Machiavelli. Moreover, it is clear from the *Diary* Bernardo kept between 1474 and 1487 that, throughout the period when his son Niccolò was growing up, Bernardo was engaged in studying several of the leading classical texts on which the renaissance concept of 'the humanities' had been founded. He records that he borrowed Cicero's *Philippics* in 1477, and his greatest rhetorical work, the *De Oratore*, in 1480. He also borrowed Cicero's most important moral treatise, the *De Officiis*, several times in the 1470s, and in 1476 he even managed to acquire his own copy of Livy's *History* – the text which, some forty years later, was to serve as the framework for his son's *Discourses*, his longest and most ambitious work of political philosophy.

It is also evident from Bernardo's *Diary* that, in spite of the large expense involved – which he anxiously itemized – he was careful to provide his son with an excellent grounding in the *studia humanitatis*.[*] We first hear of Machiavelli's education immediately after his seventh birthday, when his father records that 'my little son Niccolò has started to go to Master Matteo' for the first stage of his formal schooling, the study of Latin. By the time Machiavelli was 12 he had graduated to the second stage, and had passed into the care of a famous schoolmaster, Paolo da Ronciglione, who taught several of the most illustrious

[*] Bernardo Machiavelli, *Libro di Ricordi*, ed. C. Olschki (Florence, 1954), pp. 11, 31, 35, 58, 88, 123, 138.

humanists of Machiavelli's generation. This further step is noted by Bernardo in his *Diary* for 5 November 1481, when he proudly announces that 'Niccolò is now writing Latin compositions of his own' – following the standard humanist method of imitating the best models of classical style. Finally, it seems that – if we can trust the word of Paolo Giovio – Machiavelli may have been sent to complete his education at the university of Florence. Giovio states in his *Maxims* that Machiavelli 'received the best part' of his classical training from Marcello Adriani; and Adriani, as we have seen, occupied a chair at the university for a number of years before his appointment to the first chancellorship.

This humanist background perhaps contains the clue to explaining why Machiavelli suddenly received his governmental post in the summer of 1498. Adriani had taken over as first chancellor earlier in the same year, and it seems plausible to suppose that he remembered Machiavelli's talents in the humanities and decided to reward them when he was filling the vacancies in the chancery caused by the change of regime. It is probable, therefore, that it was owing to Adriani's patronage – together perhaps with the influence of Bernardo's humanist friends – that Machiavelli found himself launched on his public career in the new anti-Savonarolan government.

The Diplomatic Missions

Machiavelli's official position involved him in two sorts of duties. The second chancery, set up in 1437, mainly dealt with correspondence relating to the administration of Florence's own territories. But as head of this section Machiavelli also ranked as one of the six secretaries to the first chancellor, and in this capacity he was shortly assigned the further task of serving the Ten of War, the committee responsible for the foreign and diplomatic relations of the republic. This meant that, in addition to his ordinary office work, he could be called on to travel abroad on behalf of the Ten, acting as secretary to its ambassadors and helping to send home detailed reports on foreign affairs.

His first opportunity to take part in a mission of this kind came in July 1500, when he and Francesco della Casa were commissioned 'to proceed with all possible haste' to the court of Louis XII of France (L 70). The decision to send this embassy arose out of the difficulties Florence had been experiencing in the war against Pisa. The Pisans had rebelled in 1496, and over the next four years they succeeded in fighting off all attempts to crush their bid for independence. Early in 1500, however, the French agreed to help the Florentines regain the city, and dispatched a force to lay siege to it. But this too turned out disastrously: the Gascon mercenaries hired by Florence deserted; the Swiss auxiliaries mutinied for lack of pay; and the assault had to be ignominiously called off.

Machiavelli's instructions were 'to establish that it was not due to any shortcoming on our part that this undertaking yielded no results' and at the same time 'to convey the impression' if possible that the French commander had acted 'corruptly and with cowardice' (L 72, 74). However, as he and della Casa discovered at their first audience with Louis XII, the king was not much interested in Florence's excuses for her past failures. Instead he wanted to know what help he could realistically expect in the future from such an apparently ill-run government. This meeting set the tone for the whole of their subsequent discussions with Louis and his chief advisers, Florimond Robertet and the archbishop of Rouen. The upshot was that, although Machiavelli remained at the French court for nearly six months, the visit taught him less about the policies of the French than about the increasingly equivocal standing of the Italian city-states.

The first lesson he learned was that, to anyone schooled in the ways of modern kingship, Florence's governmental machinery appeared absurdly vacillating and weak. By the end of July it became obvious that the *signoria*, the city's ruling council, would need to send a further embassy to renegotiate the terms of the alliance with France. Throughout August and September Machiavelli kept waiting to hear whether the new ambassadors had left Florence, and kept assuring the archbishop of Rouen that he expected them at any minute. By the middle of October, when there were still no signs of their arrival, the archbishop began to treat these continued prevarications with open contempt. As Machiavelli reported with obvious chagrin, he 'replied in these exact words' when assured that the promised mission was at last on its way: 'it is true that this is what you say, but before these ambassadors arrive we shall all be dead' (L 168). Even more humiliatingly, Machiavelli discovered that his native city's sense of its own importance seemed to the French to be ludicrously out of line with the realities of its military position and its wealth. The French, he had to tell the *signoria*, 'only value those who are well-armed or willing to pay' and had come to believe that 'both these qualities are lacking in your case'. Although he tried making a speech 'about the security your greatness could bring to the possessions held by his majesty in Italy', he found that 'the whole thing was superfluous', for the French merely laughed at him. The painful truth, he confesses, is that 'they call you Mr Nothing' (L 126 and n.).

Machiavelli took the first of these lessons profoundly to heart. His mature political writings are full of warnings about the folly of procrastinating, the danger of appearing irresolute, the need for bold and rapid action in war and politics alike. But he clearly found it impossible to accept the further implication that there might be no future for the Italian city-states. He continued to theorize about their military and political arrangements on the assumption that they were still genuinely capable of recovering and maintaining their independence, even though the period of his own lifetime witnessed their final and inexorable subordination to the vastly superior forces of France, Germany, and Spain.

The mission to France ended in December 1500, and Machiavelli hurried home as quickly as possible. His sister had died while he was away, his father had died shortly before his departure, and in consequence (as he complained to the *signoria*) his family affairs 'had ceased to have any order about them at all' (L 184). There were also anxieties about his job, for his assistant Agostino Vespucci had contacted him at the end of October to convey a rumour that 'unless you return, you will completely lose your place in the chancery' (C 60). Shortly after this, moreover, Machiavelli came to have a further reason for wishing to stay in the vicinity of Florence: his courtship of Marietta Corsini, whom he married in the autumn of 1501. Marietta remains a shadowy figure in Machiavelli's story, but his letters suggest that he never ceased to be fond of her, while she for her part bore him six children, appears to have suffered his infidelities with patience, and eventually outlived him by a quarter of a century.

During the next two years, which Machiavelli spent mainly in and around Florence, the *signoria* became perturbed about the rise of a new and threatening military power on its borders: that of Cesare Borgia. In April 1501 Borgia was created duke of Romagna by his father, Pope Alexander VI. He thereupon launched a series of audacious campaigns designed to carve out for himself a territory to match his new and resounding title. First he seized Faenza and laid siege to Piombino, which he entered in September 1501. Next his lieutenants raised the Val di Chiana in rebellion against Florence in the spring of 1502, while Borgia himself marched north and took over the duchy of Urbino in a lightning *coup*. Elated by these successes, he then demanded a formal alliance with the Florentines and asked that an envoy be sent to hear his terms. The man selected for this delicate task was Machiavelli, who had already encountered Borgia at Urbino. Machiavelli received his commission on 5 October 1502 and presented himself before the duke at Imola two days later.

This mission marks the beginning of the most formative period of Machiavelli's diplomatic career, the period in which he was able to play the role that most delighted him, that of a first-hand observer and assessor of contemporary statecraft. It was also during this time that he arrived at his definitive judgements on most of the leaders whose policies he was able to watch in the process of being formed. It is often suggested that Machiavelli's *Legations* merely contain the 'raw materials' or 'rough drafts' of his later political views, and that he subsequently reworked and even idealized his observations in the years of his enforced retirement. As we shall see, however, a study of the *Legations* reveals that Machiavelli's evaluations, and even his epigrams, generally occurred to him at once and were later incorporated virtually without alteration into the pages of the *Discourses* and especially *The Prince*.

Machiavelli's mission to Borgia's court lasted nearly four months, in the course of which he had many discussions tête-à-tête with the duke, who seems to have gone out of his way to expound his policies and the ambitions underlying them. Machiavelli was greatly impressed. The duke, he reported, is 'superhuman in his courage', as well as being a man of grand designs, who 'thinks himself capable of attaining anything he wants' (L 520). Moreover, his actions are no less striking than his words, for he 'controls everything by himself', governs 'with extreme secrecy', and is capable in consequence of deciding and executing his plans with devastating suddenness (L 427, 503). In short, Machiavelli recognized that Borgia was no mere upstart *condottiere*, but someone who 'must now be regarded as a new power in Italy' (L 422).

These observations, originally sent in secret to the Ten of War, have since become celebrated, for they recur almost word for word in chapter 7 of *The Prince*. Outlining Borgia's career, Machiavelli again emphasizes the duke's high courage, his exceptional abilities and tremendous sense of purpose (33–4). He also reiterates his opinion that Borgia was no less impressive in the execution of his schemes. He 'made use of every means and action possible' for 'putting down his roots', and managed to lay 'mighty foundations for future power' in such a short time that, if his luck had not deserted him, he 'would have mastered every difficulty' (29, 33).

While he admired Borgia's qualities of leadership, however, Machiavelli felt an element of uneasiness from the outset about the duke's astounding self-confidence. As early as October 1502 he wrote from Imola that 'as long as I have been here, the duke's government has been founded on nothing more than his good Fortune' (L 386). By the start of the following year he was speaking with increasing disapproval of the fact that the duke was still content to rely on his 'unheard-of good luck' (L 520). And by October 1503, when Machiavelli was sent on a mission to Rome, and again had an opportunity of observing Borgia at close quarters, his earlier doubts crystallized into a strong sense of the limitations of the duke's capacities.

The main purpose of Machiavelli's journey to Rome was to report on an unusual crisis which had developed at the papal court. The pope, Alexander VI, had died in August and his successor, Pius III, had in turn died within a month of taking office. The Florentine *signoria* was anxious to receive daily bulletins about what was likely to happen next, especially after Borgia switched sides and agreed to promote the candidacy of Cardinal Giuliano della Rovere. This development looked potentially threatening to Florence's interests, for the duke's support had been bought with a promise that he would be appointed captain-general of the papal armies if Rovere were elected. It seemed certain, if Borgia secured this post, that he would begin a new series of hostile campaigns on the borders of Florentine territory.

Machiavelli's earliest dispatches accordingly concentrate on the meeting of the conclave, in which Rovere was elected 'by an enormous majority' and took the name of Julius II (L 599). But once this matter had been settled, everyone's attention shifted to the struggle that started to develop between Borgia and the pope. As Machiavelli watched these two masters of duplicity beginning to circle around one another, he saw that his initial doubts about the duke's abilities had been thoroughly justified.

Borgia, he felt, had already displayed a lack of foresight in failing to see the dangers inherent in switching his support to Rovere. As he reminded the Ten of War, the cardinal had been forced 'to live in exile for ten years' under the pontificate of the duke's father, Alexander VI. Surely, he added, Rovere 'cannot have forgotten this so quickly' that he now looks with genuine favour on an alliance with the son of his enemy (L 599). But Machiavelli's most serious criticism was that, even in this equivocal and perilous situation, Borgia continued to place an altogether hubristic reliance on his uninterrupted run of good luck. At first Machiavelli simply noted, in some apparent surprise, that 'the duke is allowing himself to be carried away by his immense confidence' (L 599). Two weeks later, when Borgia's papal commission had still not arrived, and his possessions in the Romagna had begun to rise in widespread revolt, he reported in more acid tones that the duke 'has become stupefied' by 'these blows of Fortune, which he is not accustomed to taste' (L 631). By the end of the month, Machiavelli had come to the conclusion that Borgia's ill Fortune had unmanned him so completely that he was now incapable of remaining firm in any decision, and on 26 November he felt able to assure the Ten of War that 'you can henceforth act without having to think about him any more' (L 683). A week later he mentioned Borgia's affairs for the last time, merely observing that 'little by little the duke is now slipping into his grave' (L 709).

As before, these confidential judgements on Borgia's character have since become famous through their incorporation into chapter 7 of *The Prince*. Machiavelli repeats that the duke 'made a bad choice' in supporting 'the election of Julius as pope', because 'he should never have let the papacy go to any cardinal whom he had injured' (34). And he recurs to his basic accusation that the duke relied too heavily on his luck. Instead of facing the obvious contingency that he might at some point be checked by a 'malicious stroke of Fortune', he collapsed as soon as this happened (29). Despite his admiration, Machiavelli's final verdict on Borgia – in *The Prince* no less than in the *Legations* – is thus an adverse one: he 'gained his position through his father's Fortune' and lost it as soon as Fortune deserted him (28).

The next influential leader whom Machiavelli was able to assess at first hand was the new pope, Julius II. Machiavelli had been present at several audiences at the time of Julius's election, but it was in the course of two later missions that he gained his fullest insight into the pope's character and leadership. The first of these was in 1506, when Machiavelli returned between August and October to the papal court. His instructions at that point were to keep the *signoria* informed about the progress of Julius's typically aggressive plan to recover Perugia, Bologna, and other territories previously held by the Church. The second chance arose in 1510, when Machiavelli was sent on a new embassy to the court of France. By this time Julius had resolved on a great crusade to drive the 'barbarians' out of Italy, an ambition which placed the Florentines in an awkward position. On the one hand they had no desire to offend the pope in his increasingly bellicose mood. But on the other hand they were traditional allies of the French, who immediately asked what help they could expect if the pope were to invade the duchy of Milan, recaptured by Louis XII in the previous year. As in 1506, Machiavelli thus found himself anxiously following the progress of Julius's campaigns, while hoping and scheming at the same time to preserve Florence's neutrality.

Watching the warrior pope in action, Machiavelli was at first impressed and even amazed. He started out with the assumption that Julius's plan of reconquering the papal states was bound to end in disaster. 'No one believes', he wrote in September 1506, that the pope 'will be able to accomplish what he originally wanted' (L 996). In no time at all, however, he was having to eat his words. Before the end of the month Julius had re-entered Perugia and 'settled its affairs', and before October was out Machiavelli found himself concluding his mission with the resounding announcement that, after a headlong campaign, Bologna had surrendered unconditionally, 'her ambassadors throwing

themselves at the feet of the pope and handing their city over to him'
(L 995, 1035).

It was not long, however, before Machiavelli began to feel more critical,
especially after Julius took the alarming decision to launch his slender
forces against the might of France in 1510. At first he merely expressed
the sardonic hope that Julius's boldness 'will turn out to be based on
something other than his sanctity' (L 1234). But soon he was writing in
much graver tones to say that 'no one here knows anything for certain
about the basis for the pope's actions', and that Julius's own
ambassador professes himself 'completely astounded' by the whole
venture, since 'he is deeply sceptical about whether the pope has the
resources or the organisation' to undertake it (L 1248). Machiavelli was
not yet prepared to condemn Julius outright, for he still thought it
conceivable that, 'as in the campaign against Bologna', the pope's
'sheer audacity and authority' might serve to convert his maddened
onrush into an unexpected victory (L 1244). Basically, however, he was
beginning to feel thoroughly unnerved. He repeated with obvious
sympathy a remark by Robertet to the effect that Julius appeared 'to
have been ordained by the Almighty for the destruction of the world'
(L 1270). And he added with unaccustomed solemnity that the pope
did indeed 'seem bent on the ruin of Christianity and the
accomplishment of Italy's collapse' (L 1257).

This account of the pope's progress reappears virtually unaltered in the
pages of *The Prince*. Machiavelli first concedes that, although Julius
'proceeded impetuously in all his affairs', he 'was always successful'
even in his most unrealistic enterprises. But he goes on to argue that
this was merely because 'the times and their circumstances' were 'so
in harmony with his own way of proceeding' that he never had to pay
the due penalty for his recklessness. Despite the pope's startling
successes, Machiavelli accordingly feels justified in taking an extremely
unfavourable view of his statecraft. Admittedly Julius 'accomplished
with his impetuous movement what no other pontiff, with the utmost

human prudence, would ever have accomplished'. But it was only due to 'the shortness of his life' that we are left with the impression that he must have been a great leader of men. 'If times had come when he needed to proceed with caution, they would have brought about his downfall; for never would he have turned away from those methods to which his nature inclined him' (91–2).

Between his papal legation of 1506 and his return to France in 1510, Machiavelli went on one further mission outside Italy, in the course of which he was able to appraise yet another prominent ruler at first hand – Maximilian, the Holy Roman Emperor. The *signoria*'s decision to send this embassy arose out of its concern about the emperor's plan to march into Italy and have himself crowned at Rome. Announcing this intention, he demanded a large subsidy from the Florentines to help him overcome his chronic lack of funds. The *signoria* felt anxious to oblige him if he were indeed coming; but not if not. So was he in fact going to come? In June 1507 Francesco Vettori was dispatched to find out the answer, but reported in such confusing terms that Machiavelli was sent after him with additional instructions six months later. Both men remained at the imperial court until June of the following year, by which time the proposed expedition had definitely been called off.

Machiavelli's comments on the head of the house of Hapsburg contain none of the nuances or qualifications that characterize his descriptions of Cesare Borgia and Julius II. From first to last the emperor struck Machiavelli as a totally inept ruler, with scarcely any of the right qualifications for conducting an effective government. His basic weakness, Machiavelli felt, was a tendency to be 'altogether too lax and credulous', as a result of which 'he has a constant readiness to be influenced by every different opinion' put to him (L 1098–9). This makes it impossible to conduct negotiations, for even when he begins by deciding on a course of action – as with the expedition to Italy – it is still safe to say that 'God alone knows how it will end' (L 1139). It also makes for hopelessly enfeebled leadership, because everyone is left 'in

continuing confusion' and 'nobody knows what he will do at all'
(L 1106).

Machiavelli's portrait of the emperor in *The Prince* largely reproduces
these earlier judgements. Maximilian is discussed in the course of
chapter 23, the theme of which is the need for princes to listen to good
advice. The emperor's conduct is treated as a cautionary tale about the
dangers of failing to handle one's councillors with adequate
decisiveness. Maximilian is described as so 'pliable' that, if ever his
plans 'become generally known' and are then 'opposed by those
around him', this throws him off course so completely that he is
immediately 'pulled away from them'. This not only makes him
frustrating to deal with, since 'no one ever knows what he wishes or
intends to do'; it also makes him downright incompetent as a ruler,
since 'it is impossible to rely' on any decisions he makes, and 'what he
does one day he destroys the next' (87).

The Lessons of Diplomacy

By the time Machiavelli came to record his final verdicts on the rulers
and statesmen he had met, he had reached the conclusion that there
was one simple yet fundamental lesson which they had all
misunderstood, as a result of which they had generally failed in their
undertakings, or else had succeeded more by luck than sound political
judgement. The basic weakness they all shared was a fatal inflexibility
in the face of changing circumstances. Cesare Borgia was at all times
overweening in his self-confidence; Maximilian was always cautious
and over-hesitant; Julius II was always impetuous and over-excited.
What they all refused to recognize was that they would have been far
more succcessful if they had sought to accommodate their
personalities to the exigencies of the times, instead of trying to
reshape their times in the mould of their personalities.

Machiavelli eventually placed this judgement at the very heart of his analysis of political leadership in *The Prince*. However, he first registered the insight much earlier, in the course of his active career as a diplomat. Furthermore, it is clear from his *Legations* that the generalization first struck him less as a result of his own reflections than through listening to, and subsequently thinking about, the views of two of the shrewdest politicians with whom he came into contact. The point was first put to him on the day of Julius II's election to the pontificate. Machiavelli found himself drawn into conversation with Francesco Soderini, cardinal of Volterra and brother of Piero Soderini, the leader (*gonfaloniere*) of Florence's government. The cardinal assured him that 'not for many years has our city had so much to hope for from a new pope as from the present one'. 'But only', he added, 'if you know how to harmonise with the times' (L 593). Two years later, Machiavelli met with the same judgement in the course of negotiating with Pandolfo Petrucci, the lord of Siena, whom he was later to mention admiringly in *The Prince* as 'a very able man' (85). Machiavelli had been commissioned by the *signoria* to demand the reasons for 'all the tricks and intrigues' which had marked Pandolfo's dealings with Florence (L 911). Pandolfo responded with an effrontery that evidently impressed Machiavelli very much. 'Wishing to make as few mistakes as possible,' he replied, 'I conduct my government day by day, and arrange my affairs hour by hour; because the times are more powerful than our brains' (L 912).

Although Machiavelli's pronouncements on the rulers of his age are in general severely critical, it would be misleading to conclude that he regarded the entire record of contemporary statecraft as nothing more than a history of crimes, follies, and misfortunes. At several moments in his diplomatic career he was able to watch a political problem being confronted and resolved in a manner that not only commanded his unequivocal admiration, but also exercised a clear influence on his own theories of political leadership. One such incident occurred in 1503, in the course of the protracted battle of wits between Cesare Borgia and the pope. Machiavelli was fascinated to see how Julius would cope with the dilemma raised by the duke's presence at the papal court. As he reminded the Ten of War, 'the hatred his holiness has always felt' for Borgia 'is well-known', but this hardly alters the fact that Borgia 'has been more help to him than anyone else' in securing his election, as a result of which he 'has made the duke a number of very large promises' (L 599). The problem seemed insoluble: how could Julius hope to achieve any freedom of action without at the same time violating his solemn pledge?

As Machiavelli quickly discovered, the answer came in two disarmingly simple stages. Before his elevation, Julius was careful to emphasize that, 'being a man of great good faith', he was absolutely bound 'to stay in contact' with Borgia 'in order to keep his word to him' (L 613, 621). But as soon as he felt secure, he instantly reneged on all his promises. He not only denied the duke his title and troops, but actually had him arrested and imprisoned him in the papal palace. Machiavelli is scarcely able to conceal his astonishment as well as admiration at the *coup*. 'See now', he exclaims, 'how honourably this pope begins to pay his debts: he simply cancels them by crossing them out.' Nor does anyone consider, he adds significantly, that the papacy has been disgraced; on the contrary, 'everybody continues with the same enthusiasm to bless the pope's hands' (L 683).

On this occasion Machiavelli felt disappointed with Borgia for allowing himself to be so ruinously outflanked. As he typically put it, the duke ought never to have supposed 'that the words of another are more to be relied on than his own' (L 600). Nevertheless, Borgia was undoubtedly the ruler whom Machiavelli found it most instructive to observe in action, and on two other occasions he was privileged to watch him confronting a dangerous crisis and surmounting it with a strength and assurance that earned him Machiavelli's complete respect.

The first of these emergencies arose in December 1502, when the people of the Romagna suddenly voiced their outrage at the oppressive methods used by Borgia's lieutenant, Rimirro de Orco, in pacifying the province in the previous year. Admittedly Rimirro had merely been executing the duke's orders, and had done so with conspicuous success, reducing the whole area from chaos to sound government. But his cruelty had stirred up so much hatred that the continuing stability of the province was now in jeopardy. What was Borgia to do? His solution displayed a terrifying briskness, a quality that Machiavelli mirrors in his account of the episode. Rimirro was summoned to Imola, and four days later 'he was found in the public square, cut into two pieces, where his body still remains, so that the entire populace has been able to see it'. 'It has simply been the pleasure of the duke', Machiavelli adds, 'to show that he can make and unmake men as he wants, according to their deserts' (L 503).

The other point at which Borgia evoked Machiavelli's rather stunned admiration was in dealing with the military difficulties that developed in the Romagna at about the same time. At first the duke had been obliged to rely on the petty lords of the area for his chief military support. But in the summer of 1502 it became clear that their leaders – especially the Orsini and the Vitelli – were not only untrustworthy but were plotting against him. What should he do? His first move was simply to get rid of them by feigning reconciliation, summoning them to a meeting at Senigallia and murdering them *en masse*. For once Machiavelli's studied coolness deserts him as he describes the manœuvre, and he admits to being 'lost in wonder at this development' (L 508). Next, Borgia resolved that in future he ought never to make use of such treacherous allies, but ought instead to raise his own troops. This policy – almost unheard of at a time when practically every Italian prince fought with hired mercenaries – seems to have struck Machiavelli at once as being an exceptionally far-sighted move. He reports with obvious approval that the duke has not only decided that 'one of the foundations of his power' must henceforth be 'his own arms', but has started the process of recruitment at an astonishing rate, 'having already conducted a review of five hundred men-at-arms and the same number of light cavalry' (L 419). Switching to his most admonitory style, he explains that he is 'writing this all the more willingly' because he has come to believe that 'anyone who is well-armed, and has his own soldiers, will always find himself in a position of advantage, however things may happen to turn out' (L 455).

By 1510, after a decade of missions abroad, Machiavelli had made up his mind about most of the statesmen he had met. Only Julius II continued to some extent to puzzle him. On the one hand, the pope's declaration of war on France in 1510 struck Machiavelli as almost insanely irresponsible. It required no imagination to see that 'a state of enmity between these two powers' would be 'the most terrifying misfortune that could arise' from Florence's point of view (L 1273). On the other hand, he could not resist hoping that, by sheer impetuosity, Julius might yet prove to be the saviour rather than the scourge of Italy. At the end of the campaign against Bologna, Machiavelli permitted himself to wonder whether the pope might not 'go on to something greater', so that 'this time Italy really may find herself delivered from those who have planned to engulf her' (L 1028). Four years later, despite the worsening of the international crisis, he was still trying to fight off his growing fears with the reflection that, 'as in the case of Bologna', the pope might yet manage 'to carry everyone along with him' (L 1244).

Unfortunately for Machiavelli and for Florence, his fears yielded better predictions than his hopes. After being hard pressed in the fighting of 1511, Julius reacted by concluding an alliance that changed the face of Italy. On 4 October 1511 he signed the Holy League with Ferdinand of Spain, thereby winning Spanish military support for the crusade against France. As soon as the new campaigning season opened in 1512, the formidable Spanish infantry marched into Italy. First they pushed back the French advance, forcing them to evacuate Ravenna,

Parma, and Bologna and finally to retreat beyond Milan. Then they turned against Florence. The city had not dared defy the French, and had failed in consequence to declare its support for the pope. Now it found itself paying a costly penalty for its mistake. On 29 August the Spanish sacked the neighbouring town of Prato, and three days later the Florentines capitulated. The *gonfaloniere* Soderini fled into exile, the Medici re-entered the city after an absence of eighteen years, and a few weeks later the republic was dissolved.

Machiavelli's own fortunes collapsed with those of the republican regime. On 7 November he was formally dismissed from his post in the chancery. Three days later he was sentenced to confinement within Florentine territory for a year, the surety being the enormous sum of a thousand florins. Then in February 1513 came the worst blow of all. He was mistakenly suspected of taking part in an abortive conspiracy against the new Medicean government, and after being put to the torture he was condemned to imprisonment and the payment of a heavy fine. As he later complained to the Medici in the dedication to *The Prince*, 'Fortune's great and steady malice' had suddenly and viciously struck him down (11).

Chapter 2
The Adviser to Princes

The Florentine Context

Early in 1513 the Medici family scored its most brilliant triumph of all. On 22 February Cardinal Giovanni de' Medici set out for Rome after learning of Julius II's death, and on 11 March he emerged from the conclave of cardinals as Pope Leo X. In one way this represented a further blow to Machiavelli's hopes, for it brought the new regime in Florence an unprecedented popularity. Giovanni was the first Florentine ever to become pope, and according to Luca Landucci, the contemporary diarist, the city celebrated with bonfires and ordnance for nearly a week. But in another way the development was an unexpected stroke of good fortune, for it prompted the government to declare an amnesty as part of the general rejoicing, and Machiavelli was freed.

As soon as he came out of prison Machiavelli began scheming to recommend himself to the city's new authorities. His former colleague, Francesco Vettori, had been made ambassador to Rome, and Machiavelli repeatedly wrote urging him to use his influence 'so that I may begin to receive some employment from our lord the pope' (C 244). However, it soon became clear that Vettori was unable or perhaps unwilling to help. Greatly discouraged, Machiavelli withdrew to his little farm at Sant'Andrea, in order (as he wrote to Vettori) 'to be

IL PRENCIPE DI
NICOLO MACHIAVELLI,
al Magnifico Lorenzo de Medici.

LA VITA DI CASTRVCCIO
Castracani da Lucca.

IL MODO, CHE TENNE IL DVCA
Valentino per ammazzare Vitellozzo Vitelli,
Oliuerotto da Fermo, il S. Paulo, &
il Duca di Grauina.

I RITRATTI DELLE COSE
della Francia, & dell'Alamagna.

IN VENETIA
Per Comin de Trino.
M D XLI.

2. The title-page of one of the numerous early Venetian editions of
The Prince.

at a distance from every human face' (C 5 16). From there he began for the first time to contemplate the political scene less as a participant than as an analyst. First he sent long and powerfully argued letters to Vettori about the implications of the renewed French and Spanish interventions in Italy. And then – as he explained in a letter of 10 December – he started to beguile his enforced leisure by reflecting more systematically on his diplomatic experience, on the lessons of history, and hence on the rules of statecraft.

As Machiavelli complains in the same letter, he is reduced to living 'in a poor house on a tiny patrimony'. But he is making life bearable by retreating to his study every evening and reading about classical history, 'entering the ancient courts of ancient men' in order 'to speak with them and ask them the reasons for their actions'. He has also been pondering the insights he acquired 'in the course of the fifteen years' when he 'was involved in studying the art of government'. The outcome, he says, is that 'I have composed a little book *On Principalities*, in which I delve as deeply as I can into discussions about this subject'. This 'little book' was Machiavelli's masterpiece, *The Prince*, which was drafted – as this letter indicates – in the second half of 1513, and completed by Christmas of that year (C 303–5).

Machiavelli's highest hope, as he confided to Vettori, was that his treatise might serve to bring him to the notice of 'our Medici lords' (C 305). One reason for wishing to draw attention to himself in this way – as his dedication to *The Prince* makes clear – was a desire to offer the Medici 'some token of my devotion' as a loyal subject (3). His worries on this score even seem to have impaired his normally objective standards of argument, for in chapter 20 of *The Prince* he maintains with great feeling that new rulers can expect to find 'that men whom they had regarded with suspicion in the early stages of their rule prove more reliable and useful than those whom they had trusted at first' (74). Since this contention is later flatly contradicted in the *Discourses* (236), it is hard not to feel that an element of special pleading has entered Machiavelli's analysis at this point, especially as he anxiously repeats that 'I must not fail to remind any ruler' that men who were 'content under the previous regime' will always prove 'more useful' than anyone else (74–5).

Machiavelli's main concern, however, was of course to make it clear to the Medici that he was a man worth employing, an expert whom it would be foolish to overlook. He insists in his Dedication that 'to understand properly the character of rulers' it is essential to be 'a man of the people' (4). With his usual confidence, he adds that his own reflections are likely, for two reasons, to be of exceptional value. He stresses the 'long experience of modern affairs' he has gained over 'many years' and with 'much difficulty and danger'. And he points with pride to the theoretical mastery of statecraft he has acquired at the same time through his 'continual study of ancient history' – an indispensable source of wisdom on which he has reflected 'with great care' (3).

What, then, does Machiavelli think he can teach princes in general, and the Medici in particular, as a result of his reading and experience? To anyone beginning *The Prince* at the beginning, he might appear to have little more to offer than a dry and over-schematized analysis of types of principality and the means 'to acquire them and to hold them' (42). In the opening chapter he starts by isolating the idea of 'dominion' and lays it down that all dominions are 'either republics or principalities'. He immediately casts off the first term, observing that for the moment he will omit any discussion of republics and concern himself exclusively with principalities. Next he offers the unremarkable observation that all princedoms are either hereditary or new ones. Again he discards the first term, arguing that hereditary rulers encounter fewer difficulties and correspondingly stand in less need of his advice. Focusing on new princedoms, he goes on to distinguish the 'completely new' from those which 'are like limbs joined to the hereditary state of the ruler who annexes them' (5–6). Here he is less interested in the latter class, and after three chapters on 'mixed principalities' he moves on, in chapter 6, to the topic that clearly fascinates him most of all: that of 'completely new principalities' (19). At this point he makes one further subdivision of his material, and at the same time introduces perhaps the most important antithesis in the whole of his political theory, the antithesis around which the argument of *The Prince* revolves. New princedoms, he declares, are either acquired and held 'by one's own arms and *virtus*', or else 'through the power of others and *fortuna*' (19, 22).

Turning to this final dichotomy, Machiavelli again exhibits less interest in the first possibility. He agrees that those who have risen to power through 'their own *virtú* and not through Fortune' have been 'the most outstanding' leaders, and he instances 'Moses, Cyrus, Romulus, Theseus and others of that stamp'. But he is unable to think of any modern Italian examples (with the possible exception of Francesco Sforza) and the implication of his discussion is that such outstanding *virtú* is scarcely to be expected amid the corruption of the modern world (20). He accordingly concentrates on the case of princedoms acquired by Fortune and the aid of foreign arms. Here, by contrast, he finds modern Italy full of examples, the most instructive being that of Cesare Borgia, who 'gained his position through his father's Fortune', and whose career is 'worthy to be held up as a model' to all those 'who have risen to power through *fortuna* and through the arms of others' (28).

This contention marks the end of Machiavelli's divisions and subdivisions, and brings us to the class of principalities with which he is pre-eminently concerned. By this stage it also becomes clear that, although he has taken care to present his argument as a sequence of neutral typologies, he has cunningly organized the discussion in such a way as to highlight one particular type of case, and has done so because of its local and personal significance. The situation in which the need for expert advice is said to be especially urgent is where a ruler has come to power by Fortune and foreign arms. No contemporary reader of *The Prince* could have failed to reflect that, at the point when Machiavelli was advancing this claim, the Medici had just regained their former ascendancy in Florence as the result of an astonishing stroke of good Fortune, combined with the unstoppable force of the foreign arms supplied by Ferdinand of Spain. This does not imply, of course, that Machiavelli's argument can be dismissed as having no more than parochial relevance. But it does appear that he intended his original readers to focus their attention on one particular time and place. The place was Florence; the time was the moment at which *The Prince* was being composed.

The Classical Heritage

When Machiavelli and his contemporaries felt impelled – as in 1512 – to reflect on the immense power of Fortune in human affairs, they generally turned to the Roman historians and moralists to supply them with an authoritative analysis of the goddess's character. These writers had laid it down that, if a ruler owes his position to the intervention of Fortune, the first lesson he must learn is to fear the goddess, even when she comes bearing gifts. Livy had furnished a particularly influential statement of this claim in Book XXX of his *History*, in the course of describing the dramatic moment when Hannibal finally capitulates to the young Scipio. Hannibal begins his speech of surrender by remarking admiringly that his conqueror has so far been 'a man whom Fortune has never deceived'. But this merely prompts him to issue a grave warning about the place of Fortune in human affairs. Not only is 'the might of Fortune immense', but 'the greatest good Fortune is always least to be trusted'. If we depend on Fortune to raise us up, we are liable to fall 'the more terribly' when she turns against us, as she is almost certain to do in the end (XXX.30.12–23).

However, the Roman moralists never thought of Fortune as an

inexorably malign force. On the contrary, they saw her as a good goddess, *bona dea*, and a potential ally whose attention it is well worth trying to attract. The reason for seeking her friendship is of course that she disposes of the goods of Fortune, which all men are assumed to desire. These goods themselves are variously described: Seneca emphasizes honours and riches; Sallust prefers to single out glory and power. But it was generally agreed that, of all the gifts of Fortune, the greatest is honour and the glory that comes with it. As Cicero repeatedly stresses in *De Officiis*, man's highest good is 'the attainment of glory', 'the enhancement of personal honour and glory', the acquisition of the 'truest glory' that can be won (II.9.31; II.12.42; II.14.48.).

How, then, can we persuade Fortune to look in our direction, to pour out the gifts from her cornucopia on us rather than on others? The answer is that, although Fortune is a goddess, she is still a woman; and since she is a woman, she is most of all attracted by the *vir*, the man of true manliness. One quality she especially likes to reward is thus held to be manly courage. Livy, for example, several times cites the adage that 'Fortune favours the brave.' But the quality she admires most of all is *virtus*, the eponymous attribute of the truly manly man. The idea underlying this belief is most clearly set out in Cicero's *Tusculan Disputations*, in which he lays it down that the criterion for being a real man, a *vir*, is the possession of *virtus* in the highest degree. The implications of the argument are extensively explored in Livy's *History*, in which the successes won by the Romans are almost always explained in terms of the fact that Fortune likes to follow and even wait upon *virtus*, and generally smiles on those who exhibit it.

With the triumph of Christianity, this classical analysis of Fortune was entirely overthrown. The Christian view, most compellingly stated by Boethius in *The Consolation of Philosophy*, is based on denying the key assumption that Fortune is open to being influenced. The goddess is now depicted as 'a blind power', and hence as completely careless and indiscriminate in the bestowal of her gifts. She is no longer seen as a potential friend, but simply as a pitiless force; her symbol is no longer the cornucopia, but rather the wheel of change which turns inexorably 'like the ebb and flow of the tide' (177–9).

This new view of Fortune's nature went with a new sense of her significance. By her very carelessness and lack of concern for human merit in the disposition of her rewards, she is said to remind us that the goods of Fortune are completely unworthy of our pursuit, that the desire for worldly honour and glory is, as Boethius puts it, 'really nothing at all' (221). She serves in consequence to direct our footsteps away from the paths of glory, encouraging us to look beyond our earthly prison in order to seek our heavenly home. But this means that, in spite of her capricious tyranny, Fortune is genuinely an *ancilla dei*, an agent of God's benevolent providence. For it is part of God's design to show us that 'happiness cannot consist in the fortuitous things of this mortal life', and thus to make us 'despise all earthly affairs, and in the joy of heaven rejoice to be freed from earthly things' (197, 221). It is for this reason, Boethius concludes, that God has placed the control of the world's goods in Fortune's feckless hands. His aim is to teach us 'that sufficiency cannot be obtained through wealth, nor power through kingship, nor respect through office, nor fame through glory' (263).

Boethius's reconciliation of Fortune with providence had an enduring influence on Italian literature: it underlies Dante's discussion of Fortune in canto VII of *The Inferno* and furnishes the theme of Petrarch's *Remedy of the Two Kinds of Fortune*. However, with the recovery of classical values in the Renaissance, this analysis of Fortune as an *ancilla dei* was in turn challenged by a return to the earlier suggestion that a distinction must be drawn between Fortune and fate.

This development originated in a changing view about the nature of man's peculiar 'excellence and dignity'. Traditionally this had been held to lie in his possession of an immortal soul, but in the work of

Petrarch's successors we find a growing tendency to shift the emphasis in such a way as to highlight the freedom of the will. Man's freedom was felt to be threatened, however, by the concept of Fortune as an inexorable force. So we find a corresponding tendency to repudiate any suggestion that Fortune is merely an agent of providence. A striking example is provided by Pico della Mirandola's attack on the alleged science of astrology, a science he denounces for embodying the false assumption that our Fortunes are ineluctably assigned to us by the stars at the moment of our birth. A little later, we begin to encounter a widespread appeal to the far more optimistic view that – as Shakespeare makes Cassius say to Brutus – if we fail in our efforts to attain greatness, the fault must lie 'not in our stars but in our selves'.

By building on this new attitude to freedom, the humanists of fifteenth-century Italy were able to reconstruct the full classical image of Fortune's role in human affairs. We find it in Leon Battista Alberti's *Della famiglia*, in Giovanni Pontano's treatise *On Fortune*, and most remarkably in Aeneas Sylvius Piccolomini's tract of 1444 entitled *A Dream of Fortune*. The writer dreams that he is being guided through Fortune's kingdom, and that he encounters the goddess herself, who agrees to answer his questions. She admits to being wilful in the exercise of her powers, for when he inquires, 'How long do you remain kindly to men?' she replies, 'To none for very long.' But she is far from heedless of human merit, and does not deny the suggestion that 'there are arts by which it is possible for your favour to be gained'. Finally, when she is asked what qualities she particularly likes and dislikes, she responds with an allusion to the idea that Fortune favours the brave, declaring that 'those who lack courage are more hateful than anyone else'.*

When Machiavelli comes to discuss 'Fortune's power in human affairs'

* Aeneas Sylvius Piccolomini, 'Somnium de Fortuna' in *Opera Omnia* (Basel, 1551), p. 616.

in the penultimate chapter of *The Prince*, his handling of this crucial theme reveals him to be a typical representative of humanist attitudes. He opens his chapter by invoking the familiar belief that men are 'ruled by Fortune and by God', and by noting the apparent implication that 'we have no remedy at all' against the world's variations, since everything is providentially foreordained (84). In contrast to these Christian assumptions, he immediately offers a classical analysis of liberty. He concedes, of course, that human freedom is far from complete, since Fortune is immensely powerful, and 'may be the arbiter of half our actions'. But he insists that to suppose our fate to be entirely in her hands would be 'to eliminate human freedom'. And since he holds firmly to the humanist view that 'God does not want to do everything, in order not to deprive us of our freedom and the glory that belongs to us', he concludes that roughly half our actions must be genuinely under our control rather than under Fortune's sway (84–5, 89).

Machiavelli's most graphic image for this sense of man as the master of his fate is again classical in inspiration. He stresses that 'Fortune is a woman' and is in consequence readily allured by manly qualities (87). So he sees a genuine possibility of making oneself the ally of Fortune, of learning to act in harmony with her powers, neutralizing her varying nature and thus remaining successful in all one's affairs.

This brings Machiavelli to the key question the Roman moralists had originally posed. How can we hope to forge an alliance with Fortune, how can we induce her to smile on us? He answers in precisely the terms they had already used. He stresses that she is the friend of the brave, of those who are 'less cautious and more aggressive'. And he develops the idea that she is chiefly excited by, and responsive to, the *virtus* of the true *vir*. First he makes the negative point that she is most of all driven to rage and hatred by lack of *virtú*. Just as the presence of *virtú* acts as an embankment against her onrush, so she always directs her fury where she knows 'that no dykes or dams have been built'. He even goes so far as to suggest that she only shows her power when men of *virtú* fail to stand up to her – the implication being that she so greatly admires the quality that she never vents her most lethal spite on those who exhibit it (85, 87).

As well as reiterating these classical arguments, Machiavelli gives them an unusual erotic twist. He implies that Fortune may actually take a perverse pleasure in being violently handled. He not only claims that 'fortune is a woman, and if you want to control her, it is necessary to treat her roughly'. He adds that she is actually 'more inclined to yield to men' who 'treat her more boldly' (87).

The suggestion that men may be able to take advantage of Fortune in this way has sometimes been presented as a peculiarly Machiavellian insight. But even here Machiavelli is drawing on a stock of familiar imagery. The idea that Fortune must be opposed with violence had been emphasized by Seneca, while Piccolomini in his *Dream of Fortune* had even gone on to explore the erotic overtones of the belief. When he asks Fortune 'Who is able to hold on to you more than others?', she confesses that she is most of all attracted by men 'who keep my power in check with the greatest spirit'. And when he finally dares to ask 'Who is most acceptable to you among the living?', she tells him that, while she views with contempt 'those who run away from me', she is most aroused 'by those who put me to flight'. *

If men are capable of curbing Fortune and thus of attaining their highest goals, the next question to ask must be what goals a new prince should set himself. Machiavelli begins by stating a minimum condition, using a phrase that echoes throughout *The Prince*. The basic aim must be *mantenere lo stato*, by which he means that a new ruler must preserve the existing state of affairs, and especially keep control

* Aeneas Sylvius Piccolomini, 'Somnium de Fortuna' in *Opera Omnia* (Basel, 1551), p. 616.

of the prevailing system of government. As well as sheer survival, however, there are far greater ends to be pursued; and in specifying what these are, Machiavelli again reveals himself to be a true heir of the Roman historians and moralists. He assumes that all men want above all to acquire the goods of Fortune. So he totally ignores the orthodox Christian injunction (emphasized, for example, by St Thomas Aquinas in *The Government of Princes*) that a good ruler ought to avoid the temptations of worldly glory and wealth in order to be sure of attaining his heavenly rewards. On the contrary, it seems obvious to Machiavelli that the highest prizes for which men are bound to compete are 'glory and riches' – the two finest gifts that Fortune has it in her power to bestow (85).

Like the Roman moralists, however, Machiavelli sets aside the acquisition of riches as a base pursuit, and argues that the noblest aim for 'a far-seeing and *virtuoso*' prince must be to introduce a form of government 'that will bring honour to him' and make him glorious (87). For new rulers, he adds, there is even the possibility of winning a 'double glory': they not only have the chance to inaugurate a new princedom, but also to strengthen it 'with good laws, strong arms, reliable allies and exemplary conduct' (83). The attainment of worldly honour and glory is thus the highest goal for Machiavelli no less than for Livy or Cicero. When he asks himself in the final chapter of *The Prince* whether the condition of Italy is conducive to the success of a new ruler, he treats this as equivalent to asking whether a man of *virtù* can hope to 'mould it into a form that will bring honour to him' (87). And when he expresses his admiration for Ferdinand of Spain – whom he respects most of all among contemporary statesmen – the reason he gives is that Ferdinand has done 'great things' that have made him 'the most famous and glorious king in Christendom' (76).

These goals, Machiavelli thinks, are not especially difficult to attain – at least in their minimum form – where a prince has inherited a dominion 'accustomed to the rule of those belonging to the present ruler's family' (6). But they are very hard for a new prince to achieve, particularly if he owes his position to a stroke of good Fortune. Such regimes 'cannot sufficiently develop their roots' and are liable to be blown away by the first unfavourable weather that Fortune chooses to send them (23). And they cannot – or rather, they emphatically must not – place any trust in Fortune's continuing benevolence, for this is to rely on the most unreliable force in human affairs. For Machiavelli, the next – and the most crucial – question is accordingly this: what maxims, what precepts, can be offered to a new ruler such that, if they are 'put into practice skilfully', they will make him 'seem very well established' (83)? It is with the answer to this question that the rest of *The Prince* is chiefly concerned.

The Machiavellian Revolution

Machiavelli's advice to new princes comes in two principal parts. His first and fundamental point is that 'the main foundations of all states' are 'good laws and good armies'. Moreover, good armies are even more important than good laws, because 'it is impossible to have good laws if good arms are lacking', whereas 'if there are good arms there must also be good laws' (42–3). The moral – put with a typical touch of exaggeration – is that a wise prince 'should have no other objective and no other concern' than 'war and its methods and practices' (51–2).

Machiavelli goes on to specify that armies are basically of two types: hired mercenaries and citizen militias. In Italy the mercenary system was almost universally employed, but Machiavelli proceeds in chapter 12 to launch an all-out attack on it. 'For many years' the Italians have been 'controlled by mercenary armies' and the results have been appalling: the entire peninsula 'has been overrun by Charles, plundered by Louis, ravaged by Ferdinand and treated with contempt by the Swiss' (47). Nor could anything better have been expected, for all mercenaries 'are useless and dangerous'. They are 'disunited, ambitious, undisciplined and treacherous' and their capacity to ruin you 'is only postponed until the time comes when they are required to fight' (43). To Machiavelli the implications are obvious, and he states them with great force in chapter 13. Wise princes will always 'avoid using these troops and form armies composed of their own men'. So strongly does he feel this that he even adds the almost absurd claim that they will 'prefer to lose using their own troops rather than to conquer through using foreign troops' (49).

Such an intense vehemence of tone stands in need of some explanation, especially in view of the fact that most historians have concluded that the mercenary system usually worked quite effectively. One possibility is that Machiavelli was simply following a literary tradition at this point. The contention that true citizenship involves the bearing of arms had been emphasized by Livy and Polybius as well as Aristotle, and taken over by several generations of Florentine humanists after Leonardo Bruni and his disciples had revived the argument. It would be very unusual, however, for Machiavelli to follow even his most cherished authorities in such a slavish way. It seems more likely that, although he mounts a general attack on hired soldiers, he may have been thinking in particular about the misfortunes of his native city, which undoubtedly suffered a series of humiliations at the hands of its mercenary commanders in the course of the protracted war against Pisa. Not only was the campaign of 1500 a complete disaster, but a similar fiasco resulted when Florence launched a fresh offensive in 1505: the captains of ten mercenary companies mutinied as soon as the assault began, and within a week it had to be abandoned.

As we have seen, Machiavelli had been shocked to discover, at the time of the 1500 débâcle, that the French regarded the Florentines with derision because of their military incompetence, and especially because of their inability to reduce Pisa to obedience. After the renewed failure of 1505, he took the matter into his own hands and drew up a detailed plan for the replacement of Florence's hired troops with a citizen militia. The great council provisionally accepted the idea in December 1505, and Machiavelli was authorized to begin recruiting. By the following February he was ready to hold his first parade in the city, an occasion watched with great admiration by the diarist Luca Landucci, who recorded that 'this was thought the finest thing that had ever been arranged for Florence'.[*] During the summer of 1506 Machiavelli wrote *A Provision for Infantry*, emphasizing 'how little hope it is possible to place in foreign and hired arms', and arguing that the city ought instead to be 'armed with her own weapons and with her own men' (3). By the end of the year, the great council was finally convinced. A new government committee – the Nine of the Militia – was set up, Machiavelli was elected its secretary, and one of the most cherished ideals of Florentine humanism became a reality.

One might have supposed that Machiavelli's ardour for his militia-men would have cooled as a result of their disastrous showing in 1512, when they were sent to defend Prato and were effortlessly brushed aside by the advancing Spanish infantry. But in fact his enthusiasm remained undimmed. A year later, we find him assuring the Medici at the end of *The Prince* that what they must be sure to do 'above all else' is to equip Florence with her own armies (90). When he published his *Art of War* in 1521 – his only treatise on statecraft to be printed during his lifetime – he continued to reiterate the same arguments. The whole of Book I is given over to vindicating 'the method of the citizen army' against those who have doubted its usefulness (580). Machiavelli allows, of course, that such troops are far from invincible, but he still insists on their superiority over any other type of force (585). He concludes with the extravagant assertion that to speak of a wise man finding fault with the idea of a citizen army is simply to utter a contradiction (583).

We can now understand why Machiavelli felt so impressed by Cesare

[*] Luca Landucci, *A Florentine Diary from 1450 to 1516*, trans. A. Jervis (London, 1927), p. 218.

Borgia as a military commander, and asserted in *The Prince* that no better precepts could be offered to a new ruler than the example of the duke's conduct (23). For Machiavelli had been present, as we have seen, when the duke made the ruthless decision to eliminate his mercenary lieutenants and replace them with his own troops. This daring strategy appears to have had a decisive impact on the formation of Machiavelli's ideas. He reverts to it as soon as he raises the question of military policy in chapter 13 of *The Prince*, treating it as an exemplary illustration of the measures that any new ruler ought to adopt. Borgia is first of all praised for having recognized without hesitation that mercenary leaders are dangerously disloyal and deserve to be mercilessly destroyed. And he is even more fulsomely commended for having grasped the basic lesson that any new prince needs to learn if he wishes to maintain his state: he must stop relying on Fortune and foreign arms, raise soldiers of his own, and make himself 'complete master of his own forces' (25-6, 49).

Arms and the man: these are Machiavelli's two great themes in *The Prince*. The other lesson he accordingly wishes to bring home to the rulers of his age is that, in addition to having a sound army, a prince who aims to scale the heights of glory must cultivate the right qualities of princely leadership. The nature of these qualities had already been influentially analysed by the Roman moralists. They had argued in the first place that all great leaders need to some extent to be fortunate. For unless Fortune happens to smile, no amount of unaided human effort can hope to bring us to our highest goals. As we have seen, however, they also maintained that a special range of characteristics – those of the *vir* – tend to attract the favourable attentions of Fortune, and in this way almost guarantee us the attainment of honour, glory and fame. The assumptions underlying this belief are best summarized by Cicero in his *Tusculan Disputations*. He declares that, if we act from a thirst for *virtus* without any thought of winning glory as a result, this will give us the best chance of winning glory as well, provided that Fortune smiles; for glory is *virtus* rewarded (I.38.91).

This analysis was taken over without alteration by the humanists of Renaissance Italy. By the end of the fifteenth century, an extensive genre of humanist advice books for princes had grown up, and had begun to reach an unprecedentedly wide audience through the new medium of print. Such distinguished writers as Bartolomeo Sacchi, Giovanni Pontano, and Francesco Patrizi all wrote treatises for the guidance of new rulers, all of which were founded on the same basic principle: that the possession of *virtus* is the key to princely success. As Pontano rather grandly proclaims in his tract on *The Prince*, any ruler who wishes to attain his noblest ends 'must rouse himself to follow the dictates of *virtus*' in all his public acts. *Virtus* is 'the most splendid thing in the world', more magnificent even than the sun, for 'the blind cannot see the sun' whereas 'even they can see *virtus* as plainly as possible'.*

Machiavelli reiterates precisely the same beliefs about the relations between *virtú*, Fortune, and the achievement of princely goals. He first makes these humanist allegiances clear in chapter 6 of *The Prince*, in which he argues that 'in a completely new principality, where there is a new ruler, the difficulty he will have in maintaining it' will depend basically on whether he is 'more or less *virtuoso*' (19). This is later corroborated in chapter 24, the aim of which is to explain 'Why the rulers of Italy have lost their states' (83). Machiavelli insists that they should not blame Fortune for their disgrace, because 'she only shows her power' when men of *virtú* are not prepared to resist her (84, 85). Their losses are simply due to their failure to recognize that the only 'effective, certain and lasting' defences are those based on your own *virtú* (84). The role of *virtú is* again underlined in chapter 26, the impassioned 'Exhortation' to liberate Italy that brings *The Prince* to an end. At this point Machiavelli reverts to the incomparable leaders praised in chapter 6 for their 'outstanding *virtú*' – Moses, Cyrus, and

* Giovanni Pontano, 'De principe' in *Prosatori Latini del Quattrocento*, ed. E. Garin (Milan, n.d.), pp. 1042-4.

Theseus (20). He implies that nothing less than a union of their astonishing abilities with the greatest good Fortune will enable Italy to be saved. And he adds – in an uncharacteristic moment of flattery – that the glorious family of the Medici luckily possess all the requisite qualities: they have tremendous *virtú*; they are immensely favoured by Fortune; and they are no less 'favoured by God and by the Church' (88).

It is often complained that Machiavelli fails to provide any definition of *virtú*, and even that he is innocent of any systematic use of the word. But it will now be evident that he uses the term with complete consistency. Following his classical and humanist authorities, he treats it as that quality which enables a prince to withstand the blows of Fortune, to attract the goddess's favour, and to rise in consequence to the heights of princely fame, winning honour and glory for himself and security for his government.

It still remains, however, to consider what particular characteristics are to be expected in a man of *virtuoso* capacities. The Roman moralists had bequeathed a complex analysis of the concept of *virtus*, generally picturing the true *vir* as the possessor of three distinct yet affiliated sets of qualities. They took him to be endowed in the first place with the four 'cardinal' virtues of wisdom, justice, courage and temperance – the virtues that Cicero (following Plato) had begun by singling out in the opening book of *De Officiis*. But they also credited him with an additional range of qualities that later came to be regarded as peculiarly 'princely' in nature. The chief of these – the pivotal virtue of Cicero's *De Officiis* – was what Cicero called 'honesty', meaning a willingness to keep faith and deal honourably with all men at all times. This was felt to need supplementing by two further attributes, both of which were described in *De Officiis*, but were more extensively analysed by Seneca, who devoted special treatises to each of them. One was princely magnanimity, the theme of Seneca's *On Clemency*; the other was liberality, one of the major topics discussed in Seneca's *On Benefits*.

Finally, the true *vir* was said to be characterized by his steady recognition of the fact that, if we wish to reach the goals of honour and glory, we must always be sure to behave as virtuously as possible. This contention – that it is always rational to be moral – lies at the heart of Cicero's *De Officiis*. He observes in Book II that many men believe 'that a thing may be morally right without being expedient, and expedient without being morally right'. But this is an illusion, for it is only by moral methods that we can hope to attain the objects of our desires. Any appearances to the contrary are wholly deceptive, for expediency can never conflict with moral rectitude (II.3.9–10).

This analysis was again adopted in its entirety by the writers of advice books for Renaissance princes. They made it their governing assumption that the general concept of *virtus* must refer to the complete list of cardinal and princely virtues, a list they proceeded to amplify and subdivide with so much attention to nuance that, in a treatise such as Patrizi's on *The Education of the King*, we find the overarching idea of *virtus* separated out into a series of no less than forty moral virtues which the ruler is expected to acquire. Next, they unhesitatingly endorsed the contention that the rational course of action for the prince to follow will always be the moral one, arguing the point with so much force that they eventually made it proverbial to say that 'honesty is the best policy'. And finally, they contributed a specifically Christian objection to any divorce between expediency and the moral realm. They insisted that, even if we succeed in advancing our interests by perpetrating injustices in this present life, we can still expect to find these apparent advantages cancelled out when we are justly visited with divine retribution in the life to come.

If we examine the moral treatises of Machiavelli's contemporaries we find these arguments tirelessly reiterated. But when we turn to *The Prince* we find this aspect of humanist morality suddenly and violently overturned. The upheaval begins in chapter 15, when Machiavelli starts to discuss the princely virtues and vices, and quietly warns us that 'I am well aware that many people have written about this subject', but that 'what I have to say differs from the precepts offered by others' (54). He begins by alluding to the familiar humanist commonplaces: that there is a special group of princely virtues; that these include the need to be liberal, merciful, and truthful; and that all rulers have a duty to cultivate these qualities. Next he concedes – still in orthodox humanist vein – that 'it would be most praiseworthy' for a prince to be able at all times to act in such ways. But then he totally rejects the fundamental humanist assumption that these are the virtues a ruler needs to acquire if he wishes to achieve his highest ends. This belief – the nerve and heart of humanist advice books for princes – he regards as an obvious and disastrous mistake. He agrees of course about the nature of the ends to be pursued: every prince must seek to maintain his state and obtain glory for himself. But he objects that, if these goals are to be attained, no ruler can possibly possess or fully practise all the qualities usually 'held to be good'. The position in which any prince finds himself is that of trying to protect his interests in a dark world filled with unscrupulous men. If in these circumstances he 'does not do what is generally done, but persists in doing what ought to be done' he will simply 'undermine his power rather than maintain it' (54).

Machiavelli's criticism of classical and contemporary humanism is thus a simple but devastating one. He argues that, if a ruler wishes to reach his highest goals, he will not always find it rational to be moral; on the contrary, he will find that any consistent attempt to cultivate the princely virtues will prove to be a ruinously irrational policy (62). But what of the Christian objection that this is a foolish as well as a wicked position to adopt, since it forgets the day of judgement on which all injustices will finally be punished? About this Machiavelli says nothing at all. His silence is eloquent, indeed epoch making; it echoed around Christian Europe, at first eliciting a stunned silence in return, and then a howl of execration that has never finally died away.

If princes ought not to conduct themselves according to the dictates of conventional morality, how ought they to conduct themselves? Machiavelli's response – the core of his positive advice to new rulers – is given at the beginning of chapter 15. A wise prince will be guided above all by the dictates of necessity: if he 'wishes to maintain his power' he must always 'be prepared to act immorally when this becomes necessary' (55). Three chapters later, this basic doctrine is repeated. A wise prince does good when he can, but 'if it becomes necessary to refrain' he 'must be prepared to act in the opposite way and be capable of doing it'. Moreover, he must reconcile himself to the fact that, 'in order to maintain his power', he will *often* be forced by necessity 'to act treacherously, ruthlessly or inhumanely' (62).

As we have seen, the crucial importance of this insight was first put to Machiavelli at an early stage in his diplomatic career. It was after conversing with the cardinal of Volterra in 1503, and with Pandolfo Petrucci some two years later, that he originally felt impelled to record what was later to become his central political belief: that the clue to successful statecraft lies in recognizing the force of circumstances, accepting what necessity dictates, and harmonizing one's behaviour with the times. A year after Pandolfo gave him this recipe for princely success, we find Machiavelli putting forward a similar set of observations as his own ideas for the first time. While stationed at Perugia in September 1506, watching the hectic progress of Julius II's campaign, he fell to musing in a letter to his friend Giovan Soderini about the reasons for triumph and disaster in civil and military affairs. 'Nature', he declares, 'has given every man a particular talent and inspiration' which 'controls each one of us'. But 'the times are varied' and 'subject to frequent change', so that 'those who fail to alter their ways of proceeding' are bound to encounter 'good Fortune at one time and bad at another'. The moral is obvious: if a man wishes 'always to enjoy good Fortune', he must 'be wise enough to accommodate himself to the times'. Indeed, if everyone were 'to command his nature' in this way, and 'match his way of proceeding with his age', then 'it would genuinely come true that the wise man would be the ruler of the stars and of the fates' (73).

Writing *The Prince* seven years later, Machiavelli virtually copied out these 'Caprices', as he deprecatingly called them, in his chapter on the role of Fortune in human affairs. Everyone, he says, likes to follow their own particular bent: one man proceeds cautiously, another impetuously; one forcefully, another cunningly. But in the meantime, 'times and circumstances change', so that a ruler who 'does not change his methods' will eventually 'come to grief'. However, Fortune would not change if one learned 'to change one's character to suit the times and circumstances'. So the successful prince will always be the one who moves with the times (85–6).

By now it will be evident that the revolution Machiavelli engineered in the genre of advice books for princes was based in effect on redefining the pivotal concept of *virtú*. He endorses the conventional assumption that *virtú* is the name of that congeries of qualities which enables a prince to ally with Fortune and obtain honour, glory, and fame. But he divorces the meaning of the term from any necessary connection with the cardinal and princely virtues. He argues instead that the defining characteristic of a truly *virtuoso* prince will be a willingness to do whatever is dictated by necessity – whether the action happens to be wicked or virtuous – in order to attain his highest ends. So *virtú* comes to denote precisely the requisite quality of moral flexibility in a prince: 'He must be prepared to vary his conduct as the winds of fortune and changing circumstance constrain him' (62).

Machiavelli takes some pains to point out that this conclusion opens up an unbridgeable gulf between himself and the whole tradition of humanist political thought, and does so in his most savagely ironic style. To the classical moralists and their innumerable followers, moral virtue had been the defining characteristic of the *vir*, the man of true manliness. Hence to abandon virtue was not merely to act irrationally;

it was also to abandon one's status as a man and descend to the level of the beasts. As Cicero had put it in Book I of *De Officiis*, there are two ways in which wrong may be done, either by force or by fraud. Both, he declares, 'are bestial' and 'wholly unworthy of man' – force because it typifies the lion and fraud because it 'seems to belong to the cunning fox' (I.13.41).

To Machiavelli, by contrast, it seemed obvious that manliness is not enough. There are indeed two ways of acting, he agrees at the start of chapter 18, of which 'the first is appropriate for men, the second for animals'. But 'because the former is often ineffective, one must have recourse to the latter' (61). One of the things a prince therefore needs to know is which animals to imitate. Machiavelli's celebrated advice is that he will come off best if he learns to imitate 'both the fox and the lion', supplementing the ideals of manly decency with the beastly arts of force and fraud (61). This conception is underlined in the next chapter, in which Machiavelli discusses one of his favourite historical characters, the Roman emperor Septimius Severus. First he assures us that the emperor was a man of very great *virtú* (68). And then, explaining the judgement, he adds that Septimius's great qualities were those of 'a very fierce lion and a very cunning fox', as a result of which he was 'feared and respected by everyone' (69).

Machiavelli rounds off his analysis by indicating the lines of conduct to be expected from a truly *virtuoso* prince. In chapter 19 he puts the point negatively, stressing that such a ruler will never do anything worthy of contempt, and will always take the greatest care to avoid becoming an object of hatred (63). In chapter 21 the positive implications are then spelled out. Such a prince will always stand boldly forth, either as 'a true ally or an outright enemy'. At the same time he will ensure, like Ferdinand of Spain, that he presents himself to his subjects as majestically as possible, doing 'great things' and keeping his subjects 'in a state of suspense and amazement as they await their outcome' (77).

In the light of this account, it is again easy to understand why Machiavelli felt such admiration for Cesare Borgia, and wished to hold him up – despite his obvious limitations – as a pattern of *virtú* for other new princes. For Borgia had demonstrated, on one terrifying occasion, that he understood perfectly the paramount importance of avoiding the hatred of the people while at the same time keeping them in awe. The occasion was when he realized that his government of the Romagna, in the capable but tyrannical hands of Rimirro de Orco, was falling into the most serious danger of all, that of becoming hated by those living under it. As we have seen, Machiavelli was an eyewitness of Borgia's cold-blooded solution to the dilemma: the summary murder of Rimirro and the exhibition of his body in the public square as a sacrifice to the people's rage.

Machiavelli's belief in the imperative need to avoid popular hatred and contempt should perhaps be dated from this moment. But even if the duke's action merely served to corroborate his own sense of political realities, there is no doubt that the episode left him deeply impressed. When he came to discuss the issues of hatred and contempt in *The Prince*, this was precisely the incident he recalled in order to illustrate his point. He makes it clear that Borgia's action had struck him on reflection as being profoundly right. It was resolute; it took courage; and it brought about exactly the desired effect, since it 'left the people both satisfied and amazed' while at the same time removing the cause of their hatred. Summing up in his iciest tones, Machiavelli remarks that the policy not only deserves to be 'known about' but also to be 'imitated by others' (26).

The New Morality

Machiavelli is fully aware that his new analysis of princely *virtú* raises some new difficulties. He states the main dilemma in the course of chapter 15: on the one hand 'a ruler who wishes to maintain his power must be prepared to act immorally when this becomes necessary'; but

46

on the other hand he must be careful not to acquire the reputation of being a wicked man, because this will destroy his power instead of securing it (55). The problem is how to avoid appearing wicked when you cannot avoid behaving wickedly.

Moreover, the dilemma is even sharper than this implies, for the true aim of the prince is not merely to secure his position, but is of course to win honour and glory as well. As Machiavelli indicates in recounting the story of Agathocles of Sicily in chapter 8, this greatly intensifies the predicament in which any new ruler finds himself. Agathocles, we are told, 'always lived a very dissolute life' and was known for 'appallingly cruel and inhumane conduct'. These attributes brought him immense success, enabling him to rise from 'the lowest and most abject origins' to become king of Syracuse and hold on to his principality 'without any civil strife' (30–1). But as Machiavelli warns us, in a deeply revealing phrase, such unashamed cruelties may win us power 'but not glory'. Although Agathocles was able to maintain his state by means of these qualities, they 'cannot be called *virtú*' and they 'preclude his being numbered among the finest men' (31).

Machiavelli refuses to admit that the dilemma can be resolved by setting stringent limits to princely wickedness, and in general behaving honourably towards one's subjects and allies. This is exactly what one cannot hope to do, because all men at all times 'are ungrateful, fickle, feigners and dissemblers, avoiders of danger, eager for gain', so that any ruler 'who has relied completely on their promises, and has neglected to prepare other defences, will be ruined' (59). The implication is that a prince, and above all a new prince, will often – not just occasionally – find himself forced by necessity to act contrary to humanity if he wishes to keep his position and avoid being deceived (62).

These are acute difficulties, but they can nevertheless be overcome. The prince need only remember that, although it is not necessary to have all the qualities usually considered good, it is indispensable to appear to have them (66). It is desirable to be considered liberal; it is sensible to seem merciful and not cruel; it is essential in general to appear meritorious (56, 58, 64). The solution is thus to become a great simulator and dissimulator, learning the skill of 'cunningly confusing men' and making them believe in your pretence (61).

Machiavelli had received an early lesson in the value of cunningly confusing men. As we have seen, he had been present when the struggle developed between Cesare Borgia and Julius II in the closing months of 1503, and it is evident that the impressions he carried away from that occasion were still uppermost in his mind when he came to write about the question of dissimulation in *The Prince*. He immediately refers back to the episode he had witnessed, using it as his main example of the need to remain constantly on one's guard against princely duplicity. Julius, he recalls, managed to conceal his hatred of Borgia so cleverly that he caused the duke to fall into the egregious error of believing 'that new benefits make important men forget old injuries' (29). He was then able to put his powers of dissimulation to decisive use. Having won the papal election with Borgia's full support, he suddenly revealed his true feelings, turned against the duke, and brought about his final downfall. Borgia certainly blundered at this point, and Machiavelli feels that he deserves to be blamed severely for his mistake. He ought to have known that a talent for spreading confusion is part of the armoury of any successful prince (34).

Machiavelli cannot have been unaware, however, that in recommending the arts of deceit as the key to success he was in danger of sounding too glib. More orthodox moralists had always been prepared to consider the suggestion that hypocrisy might be used as a short cut to glory, but had always gone on to rule out any such possibility. Cicero, for example, had explicitly canvassed the idea in Book II of *De Officiis*, only to dismiss it as a manifest absurdity. Anyone, he declares, who 'thinks that he can win lasting glory by pretence' is 'very much mistaken'. The reason is that 'true glory strikes deep roots and spreads its branches wide', whereas 'all pretences soon fall to the ground like fragile flowers' (II.12.43).

Machiavelli responds, as before, by rejecting such earnest sentiments in his most ironic style. He insists in chapter 18 that the practice of hypocrisy is not merely indispensable to princely government, but is capable of being sustained without much difficulty for as long as may be required. Two distinct reasons are offered for this deliberately provocative conclusion. One is that most men are so simple-minded, and above all so prone to self-deception, that they usually take things at face value in a wholly uncritical way (62). The other is that, when it comes to assessing the behaviour of princes, even the shrewdest observers are largely condemned to judge by appearances. Isolated from the populace, sustained by the majesty of his role, the prince's position is such that 'everyone can see what you appear to be' but 'few have direct experience of what you really are' (63). So there is no reason to suppose that your sins will find you out; on the contrary, 'a skilful deceiver always finds plenty of people who will let themselves be deceived' (62).

A further issue Machiavelli discusses is what attitude we should take towards the new rules he has sought to inculcate. At first sight he appears to adopt a relatively conventional moral stance. He agrees in chapter 15 that 'it would be most praiseworthy' for new princes to exhibit those qualities which are normally considered good, and he equates the abandonment of the princely virtues with the process of learning 'to act immorally' (55). The same scale of values recurs even in the notorious chapter on 'How rulers should keep their promises'. Machiavelli begins by affirming that everybody realizes how praiseworthy it is when a ruler 'lives uprightly and not by trickery' (61). He goes on to insist that a prince ought not merely to seem conventionally virtuous, but ought 'actually to be so' as far as circumstances permit. He should 'not deviate from right conduct if possible, but be capable of entering upon the path of wrongdoing when this becomes necessary' (62).

However, two very different arguments are introduced in the course of chapter 15, each of which is subsequently developed. First of all, Machiavelli is somewhat quizzical about whether we can properly say that those qualities which are considered good, but are nevertheless ruinous, really deserve the name of virtues. Since they are prone to bring destruction, he prefers to say that they 'seem virtuous'; and since their opposites are more likely to strengthen one's position, he prefers to say that they only look like vices (55).

This suggestion is pursued in both the succeeding chapters. Chapter 16, entitled 'Generosity and Meanness', picks up a theme handled by all the classical moralists and turns it on its head. When Cicero discusses the virtue of generosity in *De Officiis* (II.17.58 and II.22.77), he defines it as a desire to 'avoid any suspicion of penuriousness', together with an awareness that no vice is more offensive in a political leader than parsimony and avarice. Machiavelli replies that, if this is what we mean by generosity, it is the name not of a virtue but a vice. He argues that a ruler who wishes to avoid a reputation for parsimony will find that he 'needs to spend lavishly and ostentatiously'. As a result, he will find himself having 'to tax the people very heavily' to pay for his liberality, a policy which will soon make him 'hated by his subjects'. Conversely, if he begins by abandoning any desire to act with such munificence, he may well be called miserly at the outset, but 'eventually he will be come to be considered more generous', and will in fact be practising the true virtue of generosity (59).

A similar paradox appears in the following chapter, entitled 'Cruelty and Mercifulness'. This too had been a favourite topic among the Roman moralists, Seneca's essay *On Clemency* being the most celebrated treatment of the theme. According to Seneca, a prince who is merciful will always show 'how loath he is to turn his hand' to punishment; he will resort to it only 'when great and repeated wrongdoing has overcome his patience'; and he will inflict it only 'after great reluctance' and 'much procrastination' as well as with the greatest possible clemency (I.13.4, I.14.1, II.2.3). Faced with this orthodoxy, Machiavelli insists once more that it represents a complete misunderstanding of the virtue involved. If you begin by trying to be merciful, so that you 'overindulgently permit disorders to develop' and only turn to punishment once 'killings and plunderings' have begun, your conduct will be far less clement than that of a ruler who possesses the courage to start by making an example of the ringleaders involved. Machiavelli gives the example of his fellow Florentines, who wanted to avoid seeming cruel in the face of an uprising and in consequence acted in such a way that the destruction of an entire city resulted – an outcome hideously more cruel than any cruelty they could have devised. This is contrasted with the behaviour of Cesare Borgia, who 'was considered cruel', but whose harsh measures 'restored order to the Romagna, unifying it and rendering it peaceful and loyal' by means of his alleged viciousness (58).

This leads Machiavelli to a closely connected question which he puts forward – with a similar air of self-conscious paradox – later in the same chapter: 'whether it is better to be loved than feared, or vice versa' (59). Again the classic answer had been furnished by Cicero in *De Officiis*. 'Fear is but a poor safeguard of lasting power', whereas love 'may be trusted to keep it safe for ever' (II.7.23). Again Machiavelli registers his total dissent. 'It is much safer', he retorts, for a prince 'to be feared than loved'. The reason is that many of the qualities that make a prince loved also tend to bring him into contempt. If your subjects have no 'dread of punishment', they will take every chance to deceive you for their own profit. But if you make yourself feared, they will hesitate to offend or injure you, as a result of which you will find it much easier to maintain your state (59).

The other line of argument in these chapters reflects an even more

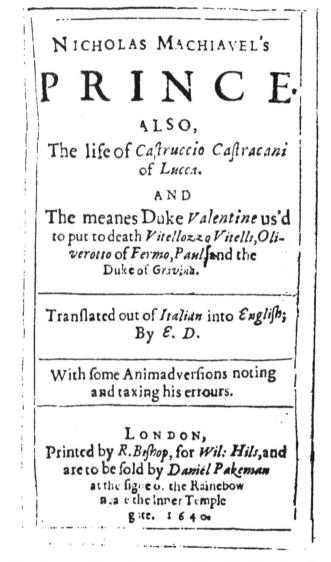

NICHOLAS MACHIAVEL'S

PRINCE.

ALSO,

The life of *Castruccio Castracani* of *Lucca.*

AND

The meanes Duke *Valentine* us'd to put to death *Vitellozzo Vitelli, Oliverotto* of *Fermo, Paul* and the Duke of *Gravina.*

Translated out of *Italian* into *English*; By *E. D.*

With some Animadversions noting and taxing his errours.

LONDON,
Printed by *R. Bishop,* for *Wil: Hils,* and are to be sold by *Daniel Pakeman* at the signe o. the Rainebow n.a e the Inner Temple gate. 1640

3. The title-page of Edward Dacres's translation of *The Prince*, the earliest English version to be printed.

scornful rejection of conventional humanist morality. Machiavelli suggests that, even if the qualities usually considered good are indeed virtues – such that a ruler who flouts them will undoubtedly be falling into vice – he ought not to worry about such vices if he thinks them either useful or irrelevant to the conduct of his government.

Machiavelli's main concern at this point is to remind new rulers of their most basic duty of all. A wise prince 'should not be troubled about becoming notorious for those vices without which it is difficult to preserve his power'; he will see that such criticisms are merely an unavoidable cost he has to bear in the course of discharging his fundamental obligation, which is of course to maintain his state (55). The implications are first spelled out in relation to the supposed vice of parsimony. Once a wise prince perceives that miserliness is 'one of those vices that enable him to rule', he will cease to worry about being thought a miserly man (57). The same applies in the case of cruelty. A willingness to act on occasion with exemplary severity is crucial to the preservation of good order in civil as in military affairs. This means that a wise prince 'should not worry about incurring a reputation for cruelty', and that it is essential not to worry about being called cruel if you are an army commander, for without such a reputation you can never hope to keep your troops 'united and prepared for military action' (60).

Lastly, Machiavelli considers whether it is important for a ruler to eschew the lesser vices and sins of the flesh if he wishes to maintain his state. The writers of advice books for princes generally dealt with this issue in a sternly moralistic vein, echoing Cicero's insistence in Book I of *De Officiis* that propriety is 'essential to moral rectitude', and thus that all persons in positions of authority must avoid all lapses of conduct in their personal lives (I.28.98). By contrast, Machiavelli answers with a shrug. A wise prince 'will seek to avoid those vices' if he can; but if he finds he cannot, then he certainly will not trouble himself unduly about such ordinary moral susceptibilities (55).

Chapter 3
The Theorist of Liberty

With the completion of *The Prince*, Machiavelli's hopes of returning to
an active public career revived. As he wrote to Vettori in December
1513, his highest aspiration was still to make himself 'useful to our
Medici lords, even if they begin by making me roll a stone'. He
wondered whether the most effective way of realizing his ambition
might be to go to Rome with 'this little treatise of mine' in order to
offer it in person to Giuliano de' Medici, thereby showing him that he
'might well be pleased to gain my services' (C 305).

At first Vettori seemed willing to support this scheme. He replied that
Machiavelli should send him the book, so that he 'could see whether it
might be appropriate to present it' (C 312). When Machiavelli duly
dispatched the fair copy he had begun to make of the opening
chapters, Vettori announced that he was 'extremely pleased
with them', though he cautiously added that 'since I do not have
the rest of the work, I do not wish to offer a final judgement'
(C 319).

It soon became clear, however, that Machiavelli's hopes were again
going to be dashed. Having read the whole of *The Prince* early in 1514,
Vettori responded with an ominous silence. He never mentioned the
work again, and instead began to fill up his letters with distracting
chatter about his latest love affairs. Although Machiavelli forced himself

to write back in a similar spirit, he was barely able to conceal his mounting anxiety. By the middle of the year, he finally came to realize that it was all hopeless, and wrote in great bitterness to Vettori to say that he was giving up the struggle. It has become obvious, he declares, 'that I am going to have to continue in this sordid way of life, without finding a single man who remembers the service I have done or believes me capable of doing any good' (C 343).

After this disappointment Machiavelli's life underwent a permanent change. Abandoning any further hopes of a diplomatic career, he began to see himself increasingly as a man of letters. The main sign of this new orientation was that, after another year or more of 'rotting in idleness' in the country, he started to take a prominent part in the meetings held by a group of humanists and literati who forgathered regularly at Cosimo Rucellai's gardens on the outskirts of Florence for learned conversation and entertainment.

These discussions at the *Orti Oricellari* were partly of a literary character. There were debates about the rival merits of Latin and Italian as literary languages, and there were readings and even performances of plays. The effect on Machiavelli was to channel his creative energies in a wholly new direction: he decided to write a play himself. The result was *Mandragola*, his brilliant if brutal comedy about the seduction of an old judge's beautiful young wife. The original version was probably completed in 1518, and may well have been read to Machiavelli's friends in the *Orti* before being publicly presented for the first time in Florence and Rome in the course of the next two years.

It is evident, however, that the most intensive debates at the *Orti* were on political themes. As one of the participants, Antonio Brucioli, later recalled in his *Dialogues*, they continually discussed the fate of republican regimes: how they rise to greatness, how they sustain their liberties, how they decline and fall into corruption, how they finally arrive at their inescapable point of collapse. Nor did their interest in civic freedom express itself merely in words. Some members of the group became such passionate opponents of the restored Medicean 'tyranny' that they were drawn into the unsuccessful plot to murder Cardinal Giulio de' Medici in 1522. One of those executed after the conspiracy misfired was Jacopo da Diacceto; among those condemned to exile were Zanobi Buondelmonti, Luigi Alamanni, and Brucioli himself. All had been prominent members of the *Orti Oricellari* circle, the meetings of which came to an abrupt end after the failure of the attempted *coup*.

Machiavelli was never so vehement a partisan of republican liberty that he felt inclined to associate himself with any of the various anti-Medicean conspiracies. But it is clear that he was deeply influenced by his contacts with Cosimo Rucellai and his friends. One outcome of his participation in their discussions was his treatise on *The Art of War*, which he published in 1521. This is actually couched in the form of a conversation set in the *Orti Oricellari*, with Rucellai introducing the argument while Buondelmonti and Alamanni serve as the chief interlocutors. But the most important product of Machiavelli's association with these republican sympathisers was his decision to write his *Discourses*, his longest and in some ways his most original contribution to the theory of government. Not only was the work dedicated to Buondelmonti and Rucellai, but Machiavelli explicitly credits them in his Dedication with having 'forced me to write what I of myself never would have written' (188).

The Means to Greatness

Machiavelli's *Discourses* nominally takes the form of a commentary on the first ten books of Livy's history of Rome, in the course of which Livy had traced the rise of the city to greatness after the defeat of her local rivals, the expulsion of her kings and the establishment of the 'free state'. But Machiavelli ranges far more widely through Livy's text than his title suggests, and handles his chosen topics in a discursive, unsystematic and occasionally even fragmentary way. Sometimes he uses Livy's narrative as a peg on which to hang a wide-ranging discussion of some major topic in the theory of statecraft, but at other times he merely talks about an individual figure or tells a story and draws a moral from it. This is by no means to say that his labyrinth lacks a guiding thread. Of the three Books into which the *Discourses* are divided, the first is primarily concerned with the constitution of a free state, the second with how to maintain effective military power and the third with questions of leadership. While I shall follow these contours, however, it needs to be remembered that the effect of doing so will be to give the impression of a more neatly organized text than Machiavelli succeeded in creating or perhaps even wanted to create.

As Machiavelli sets out to investigate the early history of Rome, there is one question that preoccupies him above all. He first mentions it in the opening paragraph of the first Discourse, and it underlies much of the rest of the book. His aim, he says, is to discover what 'made possible the dominant position to which that republic rose' (192). What enabled Rome to attain its unparalleled greatness and power?

There are obvious links between this theme and that of *The Prince*. It is true that in *The Prince* Machiavelli begins by excluding republics from consideration, whereas in the *Discourses* they furnish him with his main evidence. But it would be a mistake to infer that the *Discourses* are exclusively concerned with republics as opposed to principalities. As Machiavelli stresses in chapter 2, his interest lies not in republics as such, but rather in the government of cities, whether they are ruled 'as republics or as princedoms' (195). Moreover, there are close parallels between Machiavelli's desire in *The Prince* to advise rulers on how to attain glory by doing 'great things' and his aspiration in the *Discourses* to explain why certain cities have 'come to greatness', and why the city of Rome in particular managed to attain 'supreme greatness' and to produce such 'great results' (207–11, 341).

What, then, were 'the methods needed for attaining to greatness' in the case of Rome (358)? For Machiavelli the question is a practical one, since he endorses the conventional humanist assumption that anyone who 'considers present affairs and ancient ones readily understands that all cities and all peoples have the same desires and the same traits'. This means that 'he who diligently examines past events easily foresees future ones' and 'can apply to them the remedies used by the ancients', or at least 'devise new ones because of the similarity of the events' (278). The exhilarating hope that underlies and animates the *Discourses* is thus that, if we can find out the cause of Rome's success, we may be able to repeat it.

A study of classical history discloses, according to the start of the second Discourse, that the clue to understanding Rome's achievement can be encapsulated in a single sentence. 'Experience shows that cities have never increased in dominion or riches except while they have been at liberty.' The ancient world is said to offer two particularly impressive illustrations of this general truth. First, 'it is a marvellous thing to consider to what greatness Athens came in the space of a hundred years after she freed herself from the tyranny of Pisistratus'. But above all it is 'very marvellous to observe what greatness Rome came to after she freed herself from her kings' (329). By contrast, 'the opposite of all these things happens in those countries that live as slaves' (333). For 'as soon as a tyranny is established over a free community', the first evil that results is that such cities 'no longer go forward and no longer increase in power or in riches; but in most instances, in fact always, they go backward' (329).

What Machiavelli primarily has in mind in laying so much emphasis on liberty is that a city bent on greatness must remain free from all forms of political servitude, whether imposed 'internally' by the rule of a tyrant or 'externally' by an imperial power (195, 235). This in turn means that to say of a city that it possesses its liberty is equivalent to saying that it holds itself independent of any authority save that of the community itself. To speak of a 'free state' is thus to speak of a state that governs itself. Machiavelli makes this clear in the second chapter of his first Discourse, where he announces that he will 'omit discussion of those cities' that started by being 'subject to somebody' and will concentrate on those which began in liberty – that is, on those which 'at once governed themselves by their own judgement' (195). The same commitment is reiterated later in the chapter, where Machiavelli first praises the laws of Solon for setting up 'a form of government based on the people', and then proceeds to equate this arrangement with that of living 'in liberty' (199).

The first general conclusion of the *Discourses* is thus that cities only 'grow enormously in a very short time' and acquire greatness if 'the people are in control of them' (316). This does not lead Machiavelli to lose interest in principalities, for he is sometimes (though not consistently) willing to believe that the maintenance of popular control may be compatible with a monarchical form of government (e.g. 427). But it certainly leads him to express a marked preference for republican over princely regimes. He states his reasons most emphatically at the beginning of the second Discourse. It is 'not individual good but common good' that 'makes cities great', and 'without doubt this common good is thought important only in republics'. Under a prince 'the opposite happens', for 'what benefits him usually injures the city, and what benefits the city injures him'. This explains why cities under monarchical government seldom 'go forward', whereas 'all cities and provinces that live in freedom anywhere in the world' always 'make very great gains' (329, 332).

If liberty is the key to greatness, how is liberty itself to be acquired and kept safe? Machiavelli begins by admitting that an element of good Fortune is always involved. It is essential that a city should have 'a free beginning, without depending on anyone' if it is to have any prospect of achieving civic glory (193, 195). Cities which suffer the misfortune of starting life in a servile condition generally find it 'not merely difficult but impossible' to 'find laws which will keep them free' and bring them fame (296).

As in *The Prince*, however, Machiavelli treats it as a cardinal error to suppose that the attainment of greatness is entirely dependent on Fortune's caprice. Raising the issue at the beginning of his third Discourse, he concedes that according to some 'very weighty' writers – including Plutarch and Livy – the rise to glory of the Roman people owed almost everything to Fortune. But he replies that he is 'not willing to grant this in any way' (324). He later admits that the Romans enjoyed many blessings of Fortune, as well as benefiting from various afflictions which the goddess sent them 'in order to make Rome stronger and bring her to the greatness she attained' (408). But he insists – again echoing *The Prince* – that the achievement of great things is never the outcome merely of good Fortune; it is always the product of Fortune combined with the indispensable quality of *virtú*, the quality that enables us to endure our misfortunes with equanimity and at the same time attracts the goddess's favourable attentions. So he concludes that if we wish to understand what 'made possible the dominant position' to which the Roman republic rose, we must recognize that the answer lies in the fact that Rome possessed 'so much *virtú*' and managed to ensure that this crucial quality was 'kept up in that city for so many centuries' (192). It was because the Romans 'mixed with their Fortune the utmost *virtú*' that they maintained their original freedom and ultimately rose to dominate the world (326).

When he turns to analyse this pivotal concept of *virtú*, Machiavelli follows precisely the lines already laid down in *The Prince*. It is true that he applies the term in such a way as to suggest one important addition to his previous account. In *The Prince* he had associated the quality exclusively with the greatest political leaders and military commanders; in the *Discourses* he explicitly insists that, if a city is to attain greatness, it is essential that the quality should be possessed by the citizen body as a whole (498). However, when he comes to define what he means by *virtú*, he largely reiterates his earlier arguments, coolly taking for granted the startling conclusions he had already reached.

The possession of *virtú* is accordingly represented as a willingness to do whatever may be necessary for the attainment of civic glory and greatness, whether the actions involved happen to be intrinsically good or evil in character. This is first of all treated as the most important attribute of political leadership. As in *The Prince*, the point is made by way of an allusion to, and a sarcastic repudiation of, the values of Ciceronian humanism. Cicero had asserted in *De Officiis* that, when Romulus decided 'it was more expedient for him to reign alone' and in consequence murdered his brother, he committed a crime that cannot possibly be condoned, since his defence of his action was 'neither reasonable nor adequate at all' (III.10.41). Machiavelli insists on the contrary that no 'prudent intellect' will ever 'censure anyone for any unlawful action used in organising a kingdom or setting up a republic'. Citing the case of Romulus' fratricide, he contends that 'though the deed accuses him, the result should excuse him; and when it is good, like that of Romulus, it will always excuse him, because he who is violent to destroy, not he who is violent to restore, ought to be censured' (218).

The same willingness to place the good of the community above all private interests and ordinary considerations of morality is held to be no less essential in the case of rank-and-file citizens. Again Machiavelli makes the point by way of parodying the values of classical humanism. Cicero had declared in *De Officiis* that 'there are some acts either so repulsive or so wicked that a wise man would not commit them even to save his country' (I.45.159). Machiavelli retorts that 'when it is absolutely a question of the safety of one's country', it becomes the duty of every citizen to recognize that 'there must be no consideration of just or unjust, of merciful or cruel, of praiseworthy or disgraceful;

instead, setting aside every scruple, one must follow to the utmost any plan that will save her life and keep her liberty' (519).

This, then, is the sign of *virtú* in rulers and citizens alike: each must be prepared 'to advance not his own interests but the general good, not his own posterity but the common fatherland' (218). This is why Machiavelli speaks of the Roman republic as a repository of 'so much *virtú*': patriotism was felt to be 'more powerful than any other consideration', as a result of which the populace became 'for four hundred years an enemy to the name of king, and a lover of the glory and the common good of its native city' (315, 450).

The contention that the key to preserving liberty lies in keeping up the quality of *virtú* in the citizen body as a whole obviously raises a further question, the most basic one of all: how can we hope to instil this quality widely enough, and maintain it for long enough, to ensure that civic glory is attained? Again Machiavelli concedes that an element of good Fortune is always involved. No city can hope to attain greatness unless it happens to be set on the right road by a great founding father, to whom 'as a daughter' it may be said to owe its birth (223). A city which has not 'chanced upon a prudent founder' will always tend to find itself 'in a somewhat unhappy position' (196). Conversely, a city which can look back to 'the *virtú* and the methods' of a great founder – as Rome looked back to Romulus – has 'chanced upon most excellent Fortune' (244).

The reason why a city needs this 'first Fortune' is that the act of establishing a republic or principality can never be brought about 'through the *virtú* of the masses', because their 'diverse opinions' will always prevent them from being 'suited to organise a government' (218, 240). It follows that 'to set up a republic it is necessary to be alone' (220). Moreover, once a city has 'declined by corruption', it will similarly require 'the *virtú* of one man who is then living', and not 'the *virtú* of the masses' to restore it to greatness (240). So Machiavelli concludes that 'this we must take as a general rule: seldom or never is any republic or kingdom organised well from the beginning, or totally made over' at a later date, 'except when organised by one man' (218).

He then declares, however, that if any city is so imprudent as to rely on this initial good Fortune, it will not only cheat itself of greatness but will very soon collapse. For while 'one alone is suited for organising' a government, no government can hope to last 'if resting on the shoulders of only one' (218). The inescapable weakness of any polity that puts its trust in 'the *virtú* of one man alone' is that 'the *virtú* departs with the life of the man, and seldom is it restored in the course of heredity' (226). What is needed, therefore, for the salvation of a kingdom or a republic is not so much 'to have a prince who will rule prudently while he lives', but rather 'to have one who will so organise it' that its subsequent fortunes come to rest instead upon 'the *virtú* of the masses' (226, 240). The deepest secret of statecraft is to know how this can be done.

The problem, Machiavelli stresses, is one of exceptional difficulty. For while we can expect to find a surpassing degree of *virtú* among the founding fathers of cities, we cannot expect to find the same quality occurring naturally among ordinary citizens. On the contrary, most men 'are more prone to evil than to good', and in consequence tend to ignore the interests of their community in order to act 'according to the wickedness of their spirits whenever they have free scope' (201, 215). There is thus a tendency for all cities to fall away from the pristine *virtú* of their founders and 'descend towards a worse condition' – a process Machiavelli summarizes by saying that even the finest communities are liable to become corrupt (322).

The image underlying this analysis is an Aristotelian one: the idea of the polity as a natural body which, like all sublunary creatures, is subject to being 'injured by time' (45). Machiavelli lays particular emphasis on the metaphor of the body politic at the beginning of his third Discourse. He thinks it 'clearer than light that if these bodies are not renewed they do not last', for in time their *virtú* is certain to become corrupt, and such corruption is certain to kill them if their injuries are not healed (419).

The onset of corruption is thus equated with the loss or dissipation of *virtú*, a process of degeneration which develops, according to Machiavelli, in one of two ways. A body of citizens may lose its *virtú* – and hence its concern for the common good – by losing interest in politics altogether, becoming 'lazy and unfit for all *virtuoso* activity' (194). But the more insidious danger arises when the citizens remain active in affairs of state, but begin to promote their individual ambitions or factional loyalties at the expense of the public interest. Thus Machiavelli defines a corrupt political proposal as one 'put forward by men interested in what they can get from the public, rather than in its good' (386). He defines a corrupt constitution as one in which 'only the powerful' are able to propose measures, and do so 'not for the common liberty but for their own power' (242). And he defines a corrupt city as one in which the magistracies are no longer filled by 'those with the greatest *virtú*', but rather by those with the most power, and hence with the best prospects of serving their own selfish ends (241).

This analysis leads Machiavelli into a dilemma. On the one hand he continually stresses that 'the nature of men is ambitious and suspicious' to such a degree that most people will 'never do anything good except by necessity' (201, 257). But on the other hand he insists that, once men are allowed to 'climb from one ambition to another', this will rapidly cause their city to 'go to pieces' and forfeit any chance of becoming great (290). The reason is that, while the preservation of liberty is a necessary condition of greatness, the growth of corruption is invariably fatal to liberty. As soon as self-seeking individuals or sectarian interests begin to gain support, the people's desire to

4. Portrait of Machiavelli by Santi di Tito in the Palazzo Vecchio, Florence.

legislate 'on freedom's behalf' becomes correspondingly eroded, factions start to take over and 'tyranny quickly appears' in place of liberty (282). It follows that whenever corruption fully enters a body of citizens, they 'cannot live free even for a short time, in fact not at all' (235; cf. 240).

Machiavelli's dilemma is accordingly this: how can the body of the people – in whom the quality of *virtú* is not naturally to be found – have this quality successfully implanted in them? How can they be prevented from sliding into corruption, how can they be coerced into keeping up an interest in the common good over a sufficiently long period for civic greatness to be attained? It is with the solution to this problem that the rest of the *Discourses* is concerned.

The Laws and Leadership

Machiavelli believes that the dilemma he has uncovered can to some extent be circumvented rather than having to be directly overcome. For he allows that, while we can hardly expect the generality of citizens to display much natural *virtú*, it is not too much to hope that a city may from time to time have the good Fortune to find a leader whose actions, like those of a great founding father, exhibit an unforced quality of *virtú* in a high degree (420).

Such truly noble citizens are said to play an indispensable role in keeping their cities on the pathway to glory. Machiavelli argues that if such individual examples of *virtú* 'had appeared at least every ten years' in the history of Rome, 'their necessary result would have been' that the city 'would never have become corrupt' (421). He even declares that 'if a community were fortunate enough' to find a leader of this character in every generation, who 'would renovate its laws and would not merely stop it running to ruin but would pull it backwards', then the outcome would be the miracle of an 'everlasting' republic, a body politic with the ability to escape death (481).

How do such infusions of personal *virtú* contribute to a city's attainment of its highest ends? Machiavelli's attempt to answer this question occupies him throughout his third Discourse, the aim of which is to illustrate 'how the deeds of individuals increased Roman greatness, and how in that city they caused many good effects' (423).

It is evident that in pursuing this topic Machiavelli is still very close to the spirit of *The Prince*. So it is not surprising to find him inserting into this final section of the *Discourses* a considerable number of references back to his earlier work – nearly a dozen allusions in less than a hundred pages. As in *The Prince*, moreover, he lays it down that there are two distinct ways in which it is possible for a statesman or a general of surpassing *virtú* to achieve great things. The first is by way of his impact on other and lesser citizens. Machiavelli begins by suggesting that this can sometimes produce a directly inspiring effect, since 'these men are of such reputation and their example is so powerful that good men wish to imitate them, and the wicked are ashamed to live a life contrary to theirs' (421). But his basic contention is that the *virtú* of an outstanding leader will always take the form, in part, of a capacity to imprint the same vital quality on his followers, even though they may not be naturally endowed with it. Discussing how this form of influence operates, Machiavelli's main suggestion – as in *The Prince* and later in Book IV of *The Art of War* – is that the most efficacious means of coercing people into behaving in a *virtuoso* fashion is by making them terrified of behaving otherwise. He praises Hannibal for recognizing the need to instil dread in his troops 'by his personal traits' in order to keep them 'united and quiet' (479). And he reserves his highest admiration for Manlius Torquatus, whose 'strong spirit' and proverbial severity made him 'command strong things' and enabled him to force his fellow citizens back into the condition of pristine *virtú* which they had begun to forsake (480–1).

The other way in which outstanding individuals contribute to civic glory is more immediate. Machiavelli believes that their high *virtú* serves in itself to stave off corruption and collapse. One of his chief concerns in his third Discourse is accordingly to indicate what particular aspects of *virtuoso* leadership tend most readily to bring about this beneficial result. He begins to supply his answer in chapter 23, in which he surveys the career of Camillus, 'the most prudent of all the Roman generals' (462). The qualities that made Camillus seem especially remarkable, and enabled him to achieve so many 'splendid things' were 'his care, his prudence, his great courage' and above all 'his excellent method of administering and commanding armies' (484, 498). Later Machiavelli devotes a sequence of chapters to furnishing a fuller treatment of the same theme. He first argues that great civic leaders have to know how to disarm the envious, 'for envy many times prevents men' from gaining 'the authority necessary in things of importance' (495–6). They also need to be men of high personal courage, especially if called upon to serve in a military capacity, in which case they must be prepared – as Livy puts it – 'to show activity in the thickest part of the battle' (515). They must also possess deep political prudence, founded on an appreciation of ancient history as well as modern affairs (521–2). And finally they must be men of the greatest circumspection and wariness, incapable of being deceived by the strategies of their enemies (526).

Throughout this discussion it is clear that the fortunes of Machiavelli's native city are never far from his thoughts. Whenever he cites an indispensable aspect of *virtuoso* leadership, he pauses to indicate that the decline of the Florentine republic and its ignominious collapse in 1512 were due in large part to a failure to pay sufficient attention to this crucial quality. A leader of *virtú* needs to know how to deal with the envious: but neither Savonarola nor Soderini was 'able to overcome envy' and in consequence 'both of them fell' (497). A leader of *virtú* must be prepared to study the lessons of history: but the Florentines, who could easily have 'read or learnt the ancient habits of the barbarians', made no attempt to do so and were easily tricked and despoiled (522). A leader of *virtú* should be a man of circumspection and prudence: but the rulers of Florence showed themselves so naïve in the face of treachery that – as in the war against Pisa – they brought the republic into complete disgrace (527). With this bitter indictment of the regime he had served, Machiavelli brings his third Discourse to an end.

If we revert to the dilemma Machiavelli began by posing, it becomes evident that the argument of his third Discourse leaves it largely unresolved. Although he has explained how it is possible for ordinary citizens to be coerced into *virtú* by the example of great leadership, he has also admitted that the appearance of great leaders is always a matter of pure good Fortune, and is thus an unreliable means of enabling a city to rise to glory and fame. So the fundamental question still remains: how can the generality of men – who will always be prone to let themselves be corrupted by ambition or laziness – have the quality of *virtú* implanted and maintained in them for long enough to ensure that civic glory is achieved?

It is at this juncture that Machiavelli begins to move decisively beyond the confines of his political vision in *The Prince*. The key to solving the problem, he maintains, is to ensure that the citizens are 'well ordered' – that they are organized in such a way as to compel them to acquire *virtú* and uphold their liberties. This solution is immediately proposed in the opening chapter of the first Discourse. If we wish to understand how it came about that 'so much *virtú* was kept up' in Rome 'for so many centuries', what we need to investigate is 'how she was organised' (192). The next chapter reiterates the same point. To see how the city of Rome succeeded in reaching 'the straight road' that led her 'to a perfect and true end', we need above all to study her *ordini* – her institutions, her constitutional arrangements, her methods of ordering and organizing her citizens (196).

The most obvious question this requires us to address, according to Machiavelli, is what institutions a city needs to develop in order to avoid the growth of corruption in its 'inside' affairs – by which he means its political and constitutional arrangements (195, 295). He accordingly devotes the greater part of his first Discourse to considering this theme, taking his main illustrations from the early history of Rome, and continually emphasizing 'how well the institutions of that city were adapted to making it great' (271).

He singles out two essential methods of organizing home affairs in such a way as to instil the quality of *virtú* in the whole body of the citizens. He begins by arguing – in chapters 11 to 15 – that among the most important institutions of any city are those concerned with upholding religious worship and ensuring that it is 'well used' (234). He even declares that 'the observance of religious teaching' is of such paramount importance that it serves in itself to bring about 'the greatness of republics' (225). Conversely, he thinks that 'one can have no better indication' of a country's corruption and ruin than 'to see divine worship little valued' (226).

The Romans understood perfectly how to make use of religion in order to promote the well-being of their republic. King Numa, Romulus' immediate successor, in particular, recognized that the establishment of a civic cult was 'altogether necessary if he wished to maintain a civilised community' (224). By contrast, the rulers of modern Italy have disastrously failed to grasp the relevance of this point. Although the city of Rome is still the nominal centre of Christianity, the ironic truth is that 'through the bad example' of the Roman Church, 'this land has lost all piety and all religion' (228). The outcome of this scandal is that the Italians, through being the least religious people in Europe, have become the most corrupt. As a direct consequence, they have lost their liberties, forgotten how to defend themselves, and allowed their country to become 'the prey not merely of powerful barbarians but of whoever assails her' (229).

The secret known to the ancient Romans – and forgotten in the modern world – is that the institutions of religion can be made to play a role analogous to that of outstanding individuals in helping to promote civic greatness. Religion can be used, that is, to inspire – and if necessary to terrorize – the ordinary populace in such a way as to induce them to prefer the good of their community to all other goods. Machiavelli's principal account of how the Romans encouraged such patriotism is presented in his discussion of auspices. Before they went into battle, Roman generals always took care to announce that the omens were favourable. This prompted their troops to fight in the confident belief that they were sure of victory, a confidence which in turn made them act with so much *virtú* that they almost always won the day (233). Characteristically, however, Machiavelli is more impressed by the way the Romans used their religion to arouse terror in the body of the people, thereby inciting them to behave with a degree of *virtú* they would never otherwise have attained. He offers the most dramatic instance in chapter 11. 'After Hannibal defeated the Romans at Cannae, many citizens met together who, despairing of their native land, agreed to abandon Italy.' When Scipio heard of this, he met them 'with his naked sword in his hand' and forced them to swear a solemn oath binding them to stand their ground. The effect of this was to coerce them into *virtú*: although their 'love of their country and its laws' had not persuaded them to remain in Italy, they were successfully kept there by the fear of blasphemously violating their word (224).

The idea that a God-fearing community will naturally reap the reward of civic glory was a familiar one to Machiavelli's contemporaries. As he himself observes, this had been the promise underlying Savonarola's campaign in Florence during the 1490s, in the course of which he had persuaded the Florentines 'that he spoke with God' and that God's message to the city was that He would restore it to its former greatness as soon as it returned to its original piety (226). However, Machiavelli's own views about the value of religion involve him in departing from this orthodox treatment of the topic in two fundamental respects. He first of all differs from the Savonarolans in his reasons for wishing to uphold the religious basis of political life. He is not in the least interested in the question of religious truth. He is solely interested in the role played by religious sentiment 'in inspiring the people, in keeping men good, in making the wicked ashamed', and he judges the value of different religions entirely by their capacity to promote these useful effects (224). So he not only concludes that the leaders of any community have a duty to 'accept and magnify' anything that 'comes up in favour of religion'; he insists that they must always do so 'even though they think it false' (227).

Machiavelli's other departure from orthodoxy is connected with this pragmatic approach. He declares that, judged by these standards, the ancient religion of the Romans is much to be preferred to the Christian faith. There is no reason why Christianity should not have been interpreted 'according to *virtú*' and employed for 'the betterment and the defence' of Christian communities. But in fact it has been interpreted in such a way as to undermine the qualities needed for a free and vigorous civic life. It has 'glorified humble and contemplative men'; it has 'set up as the greatest good humility, abjectness, and contempt for human things'; it has placed no value 'in grandeur of mind, in strength of body', or in any of the other attributes of *virtuoso* citizenship. By imposing this other-worldly image of human excellence, it has not merely failed to promote civic glory; it has actually helped to bring about the decline and fall of great nations by corrupting their communal life. As Machiavelli concludes – with an irony worthy of Gibbon – the price we have paid for the fact that Christianity 'shows us the truth and the true way' is that it 'has made the world weak and turned it over as prey to wicked men' (331).

The rest of the first Discourse is largely devoted to arguing that there is a second and even more effective means of inducing people to acquire *virtú*: by using the coercive powers of the law in such a way as to force them to place the good of their community above all selfish interests.

The point is first made in broad terms in the opening chapters of the book. All the finest examples of civic *virtú* are said to 'have their origin in good education', which in turn has its origin 'in good laws' (203). If we ask how some cities manage to keep up their *virtú* over exceptionally long periods, the basic answer in every case is that 'the laws make them good' (201). The pivotal place of this contention in Machiavelli's general argument is later made explicit at the beginning of the third Discourse: if a city is to 'take on new life' and advance along the pathway to glory, this can only be achieved 'either by the *virtú* of a man or by the *virtú* of a law' (419–20).

Given this belief, we can see why Machiavelli attaches so much importance to the founding fathers of cities. They are in a unique position to act as lawgivers, and thus to supply their communities from the outset with the best means of ensuring that *virtú* is promoted and corruption overcome. The most impressive instance is said to be that of Lycurgus, the original founder of Sparta. He devised a code of laws so perfect that the city was able to 'live safely under them' for 'more than eight hundred years without debasing them' and without at any point forfeiting its liberty (196, 199). Scarcely less remarkable was the achievement of Romulus and Numa, the first kings of Rome. By means of the many good laws they enacted, the city had the quality of *virtú* 'forced upon her' with such decisiveness that even 'the greatness of her empire could not for many centuries corrupt her', and she remained 'full of a *virtú* as great as that by which any city or republic was ever distinguished' (195, 200).

This brings us, according to Machiavelli, to one of the most instructive lessons we can hope to learn from the study of history. The greatest lawgivers, he has shown, are those who have understood most clearly how to use the law in order to advance the cause of civic greatness. It follows that, if we investigate the details of their constitutional codes, we may be able to uncover the secret of their success, thereby making the wisdom of the ancients directly available to the rulers of the modern world.

After conducting this investigation, Machiavelli concludes that the crucial insight common to all the wisest legislators of antiquity can be very simply expressed. They all perceived that the three 'pure' constitutional forms – monarchy, aristocracy, democracy – are inherently unstable, and tend to generate a cycle of corruption and decay; and they correctly inferred that the key to imposing *virtú* by the force of law must therefore lie in establishing a mixed constitution, one in which the instabilities of the pure forms are corrected while their strengths are combined. As always, Rome furnishes the clearest example: it was because she managed to evolve a 'mixed government' that she finally rose to become 'a perfect republic' (200).

It was of course a commonplace of Roman political theory to defend the special merits of mixed constitutions. The argument is central to Polybius' *History*, recurs in several of Cicero's treatises, and subsequently found favour with most of the leading humanists of fifteenth-century Florence. However, when we come to Machiavelli's reasons for believing that a mixed constitution is best suited for promoting *virtú* and upholding liberty, we encounter a dramatic divergence from the conventional humanist point of view.

His argument starts from the axiom that 'in every republic there are two opposed factions, that of the people and that of the rich' (203). He thinks it obvious that, if the constitution is so arranged that one or other of these groups is allowed complete control, the republic will be 'easily corrupted' (196). If someone from the party of the rich takes over as prince, there will be an immediate danger of tyranny; if the rich set up an aristocratic form of government, they will be prone to rule in their own interests; if there is a democracy, the same will be true of the common people. In every case the general good will become subordinated to factional loyalties, with the result that the *virtú* and in consequence the liberty of the republic will soon be lost (197–8, 203–4).

The solution, Machiavelli argues, is to frame the laws relating to the constitution in such a way as to engineer a tensely balanced equilibrium between these opposed social forces, one in which all the parties remain involved in the business of government, and each 'keeps watch over the other' in order to forestall both 'the rich men's arrogance' and 'the people's licence' (199). As the rival groups jealously scrutinize each other for any signs of a move to take over supreme power, the resolution of the pressures thus engendered will mean that only those 'laws and institutions' which are 'conducive to public liberty' will actually be passed. Although motivated entirely by their selfish interests, the factions will thus be guided, as if by an invisible hand, to promote the public interest in all their legislative acts: 'all the laws made in favour of liberty' will 'result from their discord' (203).

This praise of dissension horrified Machiavelli's contemporaries. Francesco Guicciardini spoke for them all when he replied in his *Considerations on the Discourses* that 'to praise disunity is like praising a sick man's disease because of the virtues of the remedy applied to it'.[*] Machiavelli's argument ran counter to the whole tradition of republican thought in Florence, a tradition in which the belief that all discord must be outlawed as factious, together with the belief that faction constitutes the deadliest threat to civic liberty, had been emphasized ever since the end of the thirteenth century, when Remigio de' Girolami, Brunetto Latini, Dino Compagni, and above all Dante had issued fierce denunciations of their fellow-citizens for endangering their liberties by refusing to live in peace. To insist, therefore, on the astounding judgement that – as Machiavelli

* Francesco Guicciardini, 'Considerations on the "Discourses" of Machiavelli' in *Select Writings*, trans. and ed. C. and M. Grayson (London, 1965), p. 68.

expresses it – the disorders of Rome 'deserve the highest praise' was to repudiate one of the most cherished assumptions of Florentine humanism.

Machiavelli is unrepentant, however, in his attack on this orthodox belief. He explicitly mentions 'the opinion of the many' who hold that the continual clashes between the plebs and nobles in Rome left the city 'so full of confusion' that only 'good Fortune and military *virtú*' prevented it from tearing itself to pieces. But he still insists that those who condemn Rome's disorders are failing to recognize that they served to prevent the triumph of sectarian interests, and are thus 'finding fault with what as a first cause kept Rome free' (202). So he concludes that, even if the dissensions were evil in themselves, they were nevertheless 'an evil necessary to the attainment of Roman greatness' (211).

The Prevention of Corruption

Machiavelli goes on to argue that although a mixed constitution is necessary, it is by no means sufficient, to ensure that liberty is preserved. The reason is that – as he warns yet again – most people remain more committed to their own ambitions than to the public interest, and 'never do anything good except by necessity' (201). The outcome is a perpetual tendency for over-mighty citizens and powerful interest groups to alter the balance of the constitution in favour of their own selfish and factional ends, thereby introducing the seeds of corruption into the body politic and endangering its liberty.

To meet this ineradicable threat, Machiavelli has one further constitutional proposal to advance: he maintains that the price of liberty is eternal vigilance. It is essential in the first place to learn the danger signals – to recognize the means by which an individual citizen or a political party may be able 'to get more power than is safe' (265).

Next, it is essential to develop a special set of laws and institutions for dealing with such emergencies. A republic, as Machiavelli puts it, 'ought to have among its *ordini* this: that the citizens are to be watched so that they cannot under cover of good do evil and so that they gain only such popularity as advances and does not harm liberty' (291). Finally, it is then essential for everyone 'to keep their eyes open', holding themselves in readiness not only to identify such corrupting tendencies, but also to employ the force of the law in order to stamp them out as soon as – or even before – they begin to become a menace (266).

Machiavelli couples this analysis with the suggestion that there is one further constitutional lesson of major significance to be learnt from the early history of Rome. Since Rome preserved its freedom for more than four hundred years, it seems that its citizens must have correctly identified the most serious threats to their liberties, and gone on to evolve the right *ordini* for dealing with them. It follows that, if we wish to understand such dangers and their remedies, it will be advantageous for us to turn once more to the history of the Roman republic, seeking to profit from her ancient wisdom and apply it to the modern world.

As the example of Rome shows, the initial danger that any mixed constitution needs to face will always stem from those who benefited from the previous regime. In Machiavelli's terms, this is the threat posed by 'the sons of Brutus', a problem he first mentions in chapter 16 and later underlines at the beginning of his third Discourse. Junius Brutus freed Rome from the tyranny of Tarquinius Superbus, the last of her kings; but Brutus' own sons were among those who had 'profited from the tyrannical government' (235). The establishment of 'the people's liberty' thus seemed to them no better than slavery. As a result, they 'were led to conspire against their native city by no other reason than that they could not profit unlawfully under the consuls as they had under the kings' (236).

Against this type of risk 'there is no more powerful remedy, none more effective nor more certain nor more necessary, than to kill the sons of Brutus' (236). Machiavelli admits that it may appear cruel – and he adds in his iciest tones that it is certainly 'an instance striking among recorded events' – that Brutus should have been willing to 'sit on the judgement seat and not merely condemn his sons to death but be present at their deaths' (424). But he insists that such severity is in fact indispensable. 'For he who seizes a tyranny and does not kill Brutus, and he who sets a state free and does not kill Brutus' sons, maintains himself but a little while' (425).

A further threat to political stability arises from the notorious propensity of self-governing republics to slander and exhibit ingratitude towards their leading citizens. Machiavelli first alludes to this deficiency in chapter 29, where he argues that one of the gravest errors any city is liable to commit 'in keeping herself free' is that of doing 'injury to citizens whom she should reward'. This is a particularly dangerous disease to leave untreated, since those who suffer such injustices are generally in a strong position to strike back, thereby bringing their city 'all the quicker to tyranny – as happened to Rome with Caesar, who by force took for himself what ingratitude denied him' (259).

The only possible remedy is to institute special *ordini* designed to discourage the envious and the ungrateful from undermining the reputations of prominent people. The best method of doing this is 'to give enough openings for bringing charges'. Any citizen who feels he has been slandered must be able, 'without any fear or without any hesitation', to demand that his accuser should appear in court to provide a proper substantiation of his claims. If it then emerges, once a formal accusation 'has been made and well investigated', that the charges cannot be upheld, the law must provide for the slanderer to be severely punished (215–16).

Finally, Machiavelli discusses what he takes to be the most serious danger to the balance of a mixed constitution, the danger that an ambitious citizen may attempt to form a party based on loyalty to himself instead of to the common good. He begins to analyse this source of instability in chapter 34, after which he devotes most of the remainder of the first Discourse to considering how such corruption tends to arise, and what type of *ordini* are needed to ensure that this gateway to tyranny is kept closed.

One way of encouraging the growth of faction is by allowing the prolongation of military commands. Machiavelli even implies that it was 'the power citizens gained' in this way, more than anything else, that eventually 'made Rome a slave' (267). The reason why it is always 'to the detriment of liberty' when such 'free authority is given for a long time' is that absolute authority always corrupts the people by turning them into its 'friends and partisans' (270, 280). This is what happened in Rome's armies under the late republic. 'When a citizen was for a long time commander of an army, he gained its support and made it his partisan', so that the army 'in time forgot the Senate and considered him its head' (486). Then it only needed Sulla, Marius, and later Caesar to seek out 'soldiers who, in opposition to the public good, would follow them' for the balance of the constitution to be tilted so violently that tyranny quickly supervened (282, 486).

The proper response to this menace is not to take fright at the very idea of dictatorial authority, since this may sometimes be vitally needed in cases of national emergency (268–9). Rather the answer should be to ensure, by means of the right *ordini*, that such powers are not abused. This can be achieved in two main ways: by requiring that all absolute commands be 'set up for a limited term but not for life'; and by ensuring that their exercise is restricted in such a way that they are only able 'to dispose of that affair that caused them to be set up'. As long as these *ordini* are observed, there is no danger that absolute power will corrupt absolutely and 'weaken the government' (268).

The other principal source of faction is the malign influence exercised by those with extensive personal wealth. The rich are always in a position to do favours to other citizens, such as 'lending them money, marrying off their daughters, protecting them from the magistrates' and in general conferring benefits of various kinds. Patronage of this nature is extremely sinister, since it tends to 'make men partisans of their benefactors' at the cost of the public interest. This in turn serves to 'give the man they follow courage to think he can corrupt the public and violate the laws' (493). Hence Machiavelli's insistence that 'corruption and slight aptitude for free life spring from inequality in a city'; hence too his frequently reiterated warning that 'the ambition of the rich, if by various means and in various ways a city does not crush it, is what quickly brings her to ruin' (240, 274).

The only way out of this predicament is for 'well-ordered republics' to 'keep their treasuries rich and their citizens poor' (272). Machiavelli is somewhat vague about the type of *ordini* needed to bring this about, but he is eloquent about the benefits to be expected from such a policy. If the law is used to 'keep the citizens poor', this will effectively prevent them – even when they are 'without goodness and wisdom' – from being able to 'corrupt themselves or others with riches' (469). If at the same time the city's coffers remain full, the government will be able to outbid the rich in any 'scheme of befriending the people', since it will always be possible to offer greater rewards for public than for private services (300). Machiavelli accordingly concludes that 'the most useful thing a free community can bring about is to keep its members poor' (486). He ends his discussion on a grandly rhetorical note by adding that he could 'show with a long speech that poverty produces much better fruits than riches', if 'the writings of other men had not many times made the subject splendid' (488).

By the time we reach this point in Machiavelli's analysis, we can readily see that – as in his third Discourse – there is a continuing preoccupation with the fortunes of his native city lying beneath the surface of his general argument. He first of all reminds us that, if a city is to preserve its liberty, it is essential that its constitution should embody some provision against the prevalent vice of slandering and mistrusting prominent citizens. He then points out that this 'has always been badly arranged in our city of Florence'. Anyone who 'reads the history of this city will see how many slanders have at all times been uttered against citizens who have been employed in its important affairs'. The outcome has been 'countless troubles', all of which have helped to undermine the city's liberties, and all of which could easily have been avoided if only 'an arrangement for bringing charges against citizens and punishing slanderers' had at some time been worked out (216).

Florence took a further step towards slavery when she failed to prevent Cosimo de' Medici from building up a party devoted to the advancement of his family's selfish interests. Machiavelli has shown what strategy a city needs to adopt if a leading citizen tries to corrupt the people with his wealth: it needs to outbid him by making it more profitable to serve the common good. As it was, Cosimo's rivals instead chose to drive him from Florence, thereby provoking so much resentment among his followers that they eventually 'called him back and made him prince of the republic – a rank to which without that open opposition he never could have risen' (266, 300).

Florence's one remaining chance to secure her liberties came in 1494, when the Medici were again forced into exile and the republic was fully restored. At this point, however, the city's new leaders, under the direction of Piero Soderini, made the most fatal mistake of all by failing to adopt a policy which, Machiavelli has argued, is absolutely indispensable whenever such a change of regime takes place. Anyone who has 'read ancient history' knows that once a move has been made 'from tyranny into republic', it is essential for 'the sons of Brutus' to be killed (424-5). But Soderini 'believed that with patience and goodness he could overcome the longing of Brutus' sons to get back under another government', since he believed that 'he could extinguish evil factions' without bloodshed and 'dispose of some men's hostility' with rewards (425). The outcome of this shocking naïvety was that the sons of Brutus – that is, the partisans of the Medici – survived to destroy him and restore the Medicean tyranny after the débâcle of 1512.

Soderini failed to put into practice the central precept of Machiavellian statecraft. He scrupled to do evil that good might come of it, and in consequence refused to crush his adversaries because he recognized that he would need to seize illegal powers in order to do it. What he failed to recognize was the folly of yielding to such scruples when the city's liberties were genuinely at stake. He should have seen that 'his works and his intentions would be judged by their outcome', and realized that 'if Fortune and life were with him he could convince everybody that what he did was for the preservation of his native city and not for his own ambition' (425). As it was, the consequences of his 'not having the wisdom to be Brutus-like' were as disastrous as possible. He not only lost 'his position and his reputation'; he also lost his city and its liberties, and delivered his fellow-citizens over to 'become slaves' (425, 461). As in his third Discourse. Machiavelli's argument thus culminates in a violent denunciation of the leader and the government he himself had served.

The Quest for Empire

At the beginning of his second Discourse, Machiavelli reveals that his discussion of *ordini* is still only half-completed. He has so far claimed that, if a city is to achieve greatness, it needs to develop the right laws and institutions for ensuring that its citizens behave with the highest *virtú* in the conduct of their 'inside' affairs. He now indicates that it is no less essential to establish a further set of *ordini* designed to encourage the citizens to behave with a like *virtú* in their 'outside' affairs – by which he means their military and diplomatic relations with other kingdoms and republics (339). The exposition of this further argument occupies him throughout the central section of his book.

The need for these additional laws and institutions arises from the fact that all republics and principalities exist in a state of hostile competition with each other. Men are never 'content to live on their own resources'; they are always 'inclined to try to govern others' (194). This makes it 'impossible for a republic to succeed in standing still and enjoying its liberties' (379). Any city attempting to follow such an eirenic course will quickly fall victim to the incessant flux of political life, in which everyone's fortunes always 'rise up or sink down' without ever being able to 'remain fixed' (210). The only solution is to treat attack as the best form of defence, adopting a policy of expansion in order to ensure that one's native city 'can both defend herself from those who assail her and crush whoever opposes himself to her greatness' (194). The pursuit of dominion abroad is thus held to be a precondition of liberty at home.

As before, Machiavelli turns for the corroboration of these general claims to the early history of Rome. He declares in his opening chapter that 'there has never been another republic' with so many of the right *ordini* for expansion and conquest (324). Rome owed these arrangements to Romulus, her first lawgiver, who acted with so much foresight that the city was able from the outset to develop an 'unusual and immense *virtú*' in the conduct of her military affairs (332). This in turn enabled her – together with her exceptional good Fortune – to rise by a series of brilliant victories to her final position of 'supreme greatness' and 'tremendous power' (337, 341).

As Romulus correctly perceived, two fundamental procedures need to be adopted if a city is to regulate its 'outside' affairs in a satisfactory way. In the first place, it is essential to keep the largest possible number of citizens available for purposes of expansion as well as defence. To bring this about, two related policies have to be pursued. The first – examined in chapter 3 – is to encourage immigration: it is obviously beneficial to your city, and especially to its manpower, to preserve 'the ways open and safe for foreigners who wish to come to live in it' (334). The second strategy – discussed in chapter 4 – is 'to get associates for yourself': you need to surround yourself with allies, keeping them in a subordinate position but protecting them with your laws in return for being able to call upon their military services (336–7).

The other crucial procedure is connected with this preference for assembling the largest possible forces. To make the best use of them, and hence to serve the interests of your city most effectively, it is essential to make your wars 'short and big'. This is what the Romans always did, for 'as soon as war was declared', they invariably 'led their armies against the enemy and at once fought a battle'. No policy, Machiavelli crisply concludes, could be 'safer or stronger or more profitable', for it enables you to come to terms with your opponents from a position of strength as well as with the minimum cost (342).

Having outlined these military *ordini*, Machiavelli proceeds to consider a series of more specific lessons about the conduct of warfare which he believes can be learnt from a study of Rome's achievement. This topic, introduced in chapter 10, occupies him for the rest of the second Discourse, as well as being taken up – in a more polished but essentially similar style – in the central sections of his later treatise on *The Art of War*.

It is perhaps an index of Machiavelli's growing pessimism about the prospects of reviving ancient military *virtú* in the modern world that all his conclusions in these chapters are presented in a negative form. Rather than considering what approaches serve to encourage *virtú* and promote greatness, he concentrates entirely on those tactics and strategies which embody mistakes and in consequence bring 'death and ruin' instead of victory (377–8). The result is a long list of admonitions and caveats. It is imprudent to accept the common maxim that 'riches are the sinews of war' (348–9). It is injurious to make either 'hesitating decisions' or 'slow and late ones' (361). It is entirely false to suppose that the conduct of warfare 'will be turned over, in course of time, to the artillery' (367, 371). It is valueless to employ auxiliary or mercenary soldiers – an argument which, as Machiavelli reminds us, he has already presented 'at length in another work' (381). It is useless in time of war, and in peacetime it is actively harmful, to rely on fortresses as a principal system of defence (394). It is dangerous to make it impossible for a citizen to be 'avenged to his satisfaction' if he feels insulted or injured (405). And it is the worst mistake of all 'to refuse every agreement' when attacked by superior forces, and try instead to defeat them against the odds (403).

The reason Machiavelli gives for condemning these practices is the same in every case. They all fail to recognize that, if civic glory is to be attained, the quality that needs most of all to be instilled in one's own armies – and reckoned with in the armies of one's enemies – is that of *virtú*, the willingness to set aside all considerations of personal safety and interest in order to defend the liberties of one's native land.

With some of the policies he lists, Machiavelli argues that the danger involved is that of raising up exceptional *virtú* against those who practise them. This, for example, is why it is a mistake to rely on fortresses. The security they afford you makes you 'quicker and less hesitant about oppressing your subjects', but this in turn 'stirs them up in such a way that your fortress, which is the cause of it, cannot then defend you' against their hatred and rage (393). The same applies to the refusal to avenge injuries. If a citizen feels himself gravely insulted, he may derive such *virtú* from his sense of outrage that he inflicts a desperate injury by way of return, as happened in the case of Pausanias, who assassinated Philip of Macedon for denying him vengeance after he had been dishonoured (405–6).

The danger in other cases is that your fortunes may fall into the hands of people lacking in any *virtuoso* concern for the public interest. This is what happens if you allow political decisions to be made in a slow or hesitating way. For it is generally safe to assume that those who wish to prevent a conclusion from being reached are 'moved by selfish passion' and are really trying 'to bring down the government' (361). The same is true of using auxiliary or mercenary troops. Since such forces are always completely corrupt, they 'usually plunder the one who has hired them as much as the one against whom they have been hired' (382).

Most dangerous of all is the failure to appreciate that the quality of *virtú* matters more than anything else in military just as in civil affairs. This is why it is so ruinous to measure your enemies by their wealth, for what you ought to be measuring is obviously their *virtú*, since 'war is made with steel and not with gold' (350). So too with relying on artillery to win your battles. Machiavelli concedes, of course, that the Romans 'would have made their gains more quickly if there had been guns in those times' (370). But he persists in thinking it a cardinal error to suppose that, 'as a result of these fire-weapons, men cannot use and show their *virtú* as they could in antiquity' (367). He therefore continues to draw the somewhat optimistic conclusion that, although 'artillery is useful in an army where the *virtú* of the ancients is combined with it', it still remains 'quite useless against a *virtuoso* army' (372). Finally, the same considerations explain why it is especially dangerous to refuse negotiations in the face of superior forces. This is to ask more than can realistically be demanded even of the most *virtuosi* troops, and is thus 'to turn the outcome over' to 'the pleasure of Fortune' in a way that 'no prudent man risks unless he must' (403).

As in both his other Discourses, Machiavelli's survey of Roman history prompts him to end with an agonized comparison between the total corruption of his native city and the exemplary *virtú* of the ancient world. The Florentines could easily 'have seen the means the Romans used' in their military affairs, 'and could have followed their example' (380). But in fact they have taken no account of Roman methods, and in consequence have fallen into every conceivable trap (339). The Romans understood perfectly the dangers of acting indecisively. But Florence's leaders have never grasped this obvious lesson of history, as a result of which they have brought 'damage and disgrace to our republic' (361). The Romans always recognized the uselessness of mercenary and auxiliary troops. But the Florentines, together with many other republics and principalities, are still needlessly humiliated by their reliance on these corrupt and cowardly forces (383). The Romans saw that, in keeping watch over their associates, a policy of 'building fortresses as a bridle to keep them faithful' would only breed resentment and insecurity. By contrast, 'it is a saying in Florence, brought forward by our wise men, that Pisa and other like cities must be held with fortresses' (392). Finally – with the greatest anguish – Machiavelli comes to the gambit he has already stigmatized as the most irrational of all, that of refusing to negotiate when confronted by superior forces. All the evidence of ancient history shows that this is to tempt Fortune in the most reckless way. Yet this is exactly what the Florentines did when Ferdinand's armies invaded in the summer of 1512. As soon as the Spanish crossed the border, they found themselves short of food and tried to arrange a truce. But 'the people of Florence, made haughty by this, did not accept it' (403). The immediate result was the sack of Prato, the surrender of Florence, the collapse of the republic, and the restoration of the Medicean tyranny – all of which could easily have been avoided. As before, Machiavelli feels driven to conclude on a note of almost despairing anger at the follies of the regime he himself had served.

Chapter 4
The Historian of Florence

The Purpose of History

Shortly after the completion of the *Discourses*, a sudden turn of Fortune's wheel at last brought Machiavelli the patronage he had always craved from the Medicean government. Lorenzo de' Medici – to whom he had rededicated *The Prince* after the death of Giuliano in 1516 – died prematurely three years later. He was succeeded in the control of Florentine affairs by his cousin, Cardinal Giulio, soon to be elected pope as Clement VII. The cardinal happened to be related to one of Machiavelli's closest friends, Lorenzo Strozzi, to whom Machiavelli later dedicated his *Art of War*. As a result of this connection, Machiavelli managed to gain an introduction to the Medicean court in March 1520, and soon afterwards he received a hint that some employment – literary even if not diplomatic – might be found for him. Nor were his expectations disappointed, for in November of the same year he obtained a formal commission from the Medici to write the history of Florence.

The composition of *The History of Florence* occupied Machiavelli almost for the rest of his life. It is his longest and most leisured work, as well as being the one in which he follows the literary prescriptions of his favourite classical authorities with the greatest care. The two basic tenets of classical – and hence of humanist – historiography were that

5. Machiavelli's writing desk in his house in Sant' Andrea in Percussina, south of Florence, where he composed *The Prince* in 1513.

works of history should inculcate moral lessons, and that their materials should therefore be selected and organized in such a way as to highlight the proper lessons with maximum force. Sallust, for example, had offered an influential statement of both these principles. In *The War with Jugurtha* he had argued that the aim of the historian must be to reflect on the past in a 'useful' and 'serviceable' way (IV.1–3). And in *The War with Catiline* he had drawn the inference that the correct approach must therefore consist of 'selecting such portions' as seem 'worthy of record', and not trying to furnish a complete chronicle of events (IV.2).

Machiavelli is assiduous about meeting both these requirements, as he reveals in particular in his handling of the various transitions and climaxes of his narrative. Book II, for example, ends with an edifying account of how the duke of Athens came to rule Florence as a tyrant in

1342 and was driven from power in the course of the following year. Book III then switches almost directly to the next revealing episode – the revolt of the Ciompi in 1378 – after a bare sketch of the intervening half-century. Similarly, Book III concludes with a description of the reaction following the revolution of 1378, and Book IV opens after a gap of another forty years with a discussion of how the Medici managed to rise to power.

A further tenet of humanist historical writing was that, in order to convey the most salutary lessons in the most memorable fashion, the historian must cultivate a commanding rhetorical style. As Sallust had declared at the start of *The War with Catiline*, the special challenge of history lies in the fact that 'the style and diction must be equal to the deeds recorded' (III.2). Machiavelli again takes this ideal very seriously, so much so that in the summer of 1520 he decided to compose a stylistic 'model' for a history, the draft of which he circulated among his friends from the *Orti Oricellari* in order to solicit their comments on his approach. He chose as his theme the biography of Castruccio Castracani, the early fourteenth-century tyrant of Lucca. But the details of Castruccio's life – some of which Machiavelli simply invents – are of less interest to him than the business of selecting and arranging them in an elevated and instructive way. The opening description of Castruccio's birth as a foundling is fictitious, but it offers Machiavelli the chance to write a grand declamation on the power of Fortune in human affairs (533–4). The moment when the young Castruccio – who was educated by a priest – first begins 'to busy himself with weapons' similarly gives Machiavelli an opportunity to present a version of the classic debate about the rival attractions of letters and arms (535–6). The dying oration pronounced by the remorseful tyrant is again in the best traditions of ancient historiography (553–4). And the story is rounded off with numerous instances of Castruccio's epigrammatic wit, most of which are in fact stolen directly from Diogenes Laertius' *Lives of the Philosophers* and are simply inserted for rhetorical effect (555–9).

When Machiavelli sent this *Life of Castruccio* to his friends Alamanni and Buondelmonti, they accepted it very much in the spirit of a rehearsal for the large-scale historical work that Machiavelli was by then hoping to write. Replying in a letter of September 1520, Buondelmonti spoke of the *Life* as 'a model for your history' and added that for this reason he thought it best to comment on the manuscript 'mainly from the point of view of language and style'. He reserved his highest praise for its rhetorical flights, saying that he enjoyed the invented deathbed oration 'more than anything else'. And he told Machiavelli what he must have wanted most of all to hear as he prepared to venture into this new literary field: 'it seems to all of us that you ought now to set to work to write your History with all diligence' (C 394–5).

When Machiavelli duly settled down to compose his History a few months later, these stylistic devices were elaborately put to work. The book is conceived in his most aphoristic and antithetical manner, with all the major themes of his political theory reappearing in rhetorical dress. In Book II, for example, one of the *signori* is made to confront the duke of Athens with a passionate oration on 'the name of liberty, which no force crushes, no time wears away, and no gain counterbalances' (1124). In the next book one of the ordinary citizens declaims an equally lofty speech to the *signori* on the theme of *virtù* and corruption, and on the obligation of every citizen to serve the public interest at all times (1145–8). And in Book V Rinaldo degli Albizzi attempts to enlist the help of the duke of Milan against the growing power of the Medici with a further declamation on *virtù*, corruption, and the patriotic duty to offer one's allegiance to a city that 'loves all her people equally', and not to one that, 'neglecting all the others, bows down before a very few of them' (1242).

The most important precept the humanists learned from their classical authorities was that historians must focus their attention on the finest achievements of our ancestors, thereby encouraging us to emulate their noblest and most glorious deeds. Although the great Roman historians had tended to be pessimistic in outlook, and had frequently dilated on the growing corruption of the world, this had usually prompted them to insist all the more vehemently on the historian's obligation to recall us to better days. As Sallust explains in *The War with Jugurtha*, it is only by keeping alive 'the memory of great deeds' that we can hope to kindle 'in the breasts of noble men' the kind of ambition 'that cannot be quelled until they by their own *virtus* have equalled the fame and glory of their forefathers' (IV.6). Moreover, it was this feeling for the panegyric quality of the historian's task that the humanists of the Renaissance chiefly carried away from their study of Livy, Sallust, and their contemporaries. This can clearly be seen, for example, in the account of the purpose of history that appears in the Dedication to the *History of the Florentine People* which the chancellor Poggio Bracciolini completed in the 1450s. This affirms that 'the great usefulness of a really truthful history' lies in the fact that 'we are able to observe what can be achieved by the *virtus* of the most outstanding men'. We see how they come to be activated by a desire 'for glory, for their country's liberty, for the good of their children, the gods and all humane things'. And we find ourselves 'so greatly roused up' by their wonderful example that 'it is as if they spur us on' to rival their greatness.[*]

There is no doubt that Machiavelli was fully aware of this further aspect of humanist historiography, for he even refers admiringly to Poggio's work in the Preface to his own *History* (1031). But at this point – after following the humanist approach with such exactitude – he suddenly shatters the expectations he has built up. At the beginning of Book V, when he turns to examine the history of Florence over the preceding century, he announces that 'the things done by our princes, abroad and at home, cannot, like those of the ancients, be read of with

[*] Poggio Bracciolini, 'Historiae Florentini Populi' in *Opera Omnia*, ed. R. Fubini, 4 vols (Turin, 1964), II, 91–4.

wonder because of their *virtú* and greatness'. It is simply not possible to 'tell of the bravery of soldiers or the *virtú* of generals or the love of citizens for their country'. We can only tell of an increasingly corrupt world in which we see 'with what tricks and schemes the princes, the soldiers, the heads of the republics, in order to keep that reputation which they did not deserve, carried on their affairs'. Machiavelli thus engineers a complete reversal of prevailing assumptions about the purpose of history: instead of recounting a story that 'kindles free spirits to imitation', he hopes to 'kindle such spirits to avoid and get rid of present abuses' (1233).

The entire *History of Florence* is thus organized around the theme of decline and fall. Book I describes the collapse of the Roman Empire in the west and the coming of the barbarians to Italy. The end of Book I and the beginning of Book II relate how 'new cities and new dominions born among the Roman ruins showed such *virtú*' that 'they freed Italy and defended her from the barbarians' (1233). But after this brief period of modest success, Machiavelli presents the rest of his narrative – from the middle of Book II to the end of Book VIII, where he brings the story to a close in the 1490s – as a history of progressive corruption and collapse. The nadir is reached in 1494, when the ultimate humiliation occurred: Italy 'put herself back into slavery' under the barbarians she had originally succeeded in driving out (1233).

The Decline and Fall of Florence

The overriding theme of the *History of Florence* is corruption. Machiavelli describes how its malign influence seized hold of Florence, strangled its liberty, and finally brought it to tyranny and disgrace. As in the *Discourses* – which he follows closely – he sees two principal areas in which the spirit of corruption is prone to arise, and after drawing a distinction between them in the Preface he employs it to organize the whole of his account. First there is a perennial danger of corruption in the handling of 'external' policies, the main symptom of which will be a tendency for military affairs to be conducted with increasing indecision and cowardice. And secondly, there is a similar danger in relation to 'the things done at home', where the growth of corruption will mainly be reflected in the form of 'civil strife and internal hostilities' (1030–1).

Machiavelli takes up the first of these issues in Books V and VI, in which he chiefly deals with the history of Florence's external affairs. However, he does not undertake – as he had done in the *Discourses* – to provide a detailed analysis of the city's strategic miscalculations and mistakes. He contents himself with offering a series of mocking illustrations of Florentine military incompetence. This enables him to preserve the accepted format of humanist histories – in which there were always elaborate accounts of notable battles – while at the same time parodying their contents. The point of Machiavelli's military set pieces is that all the engagements he describes are wholly ridiculous, not martial or glorious at all. When, for example, he writes about the great battle of Zagonara, which was fought in 1424 at the start of the war against Milan, he first observes that this was regarded at the time as a massive defeat for Florence, and was 'reported everywhere in Italy'. He then adds that nobody died in the action except three Florentines who, 'falling from their horses, were drowned in the mud' (1193). Later he accords the same satirical treatment to the famous victory won by the Florentines at Anghiari in 1440. Throughout this long fight, he remarks, 'not more than one man died, and he perished not from wounds or any honourable blow, but by falling from his horse and being trampled on' (1280).

The rest of the *History* is devoted to the miserable tale of Florence's increasing corruption at home. When Machiavelli turns to this topic at the start of Book III, he first makes it clear that, in speaking of internal corruption, what he chiefly has in mind – as in the *Discourses* – is the tendency for civic laws and institutions to be 'planned not for the common profit' but rather for individual or sectarian advantage (1140).

He criticizes his great predecessors, Bruni and Poggio, for failing to pay due attention to this danger in their histories of Florence (1031). And he justifies his own intense preoccupation with the theme by insisting that the enmities which arise when a community loses its *virtú* in this way 'bring about all the evils that spring up in cities' – as the sad case of Florence amply demonstrates (1140).

Machiavelli begins by conceding that there will always be 'serious and natural enmities between the people and the nobles' in any city, because of 'the latter's wish to rule and the former's not to be enthralled' (1140). As in the *Discourses*, he is far from supposing that all such hostilities are to be avoided. He repeats his previous contention that 'some divisions harm republics and some divisions benefit them. Those do harm that are accompanied with factions and partisans; those bring benefit that are kept up without factions and partisans.' So the aim of a prudent legislator should not be to 'provide that there will be no enmities'; it should only be to ensure 'that there will be no factions' based on the enmities that inevitably arise (1336).

In Florence, however, the hostilities that have developed have always been 'those of factions' (1337). As a result, the city has been one of those unfortunate communities which have been condemned to oscillate between two equally ruinous poles, varying 'not between liberty and slavery' but rather 'between slavery and licence'. The common people have been 'the promoters of licence' while the nobility have been 'the promoters of slavery'. The helpless city has in consequence staggered 'from the tyrannical form to the licentious, and from that back to the other', both parties having such powerful enemies that neither has been able to impose stability for any length of time (1187).

To Machiavelli, the internal history of Florence since the thirteenth century thus appears as a series of hectic movements between these two extremes, in the course of which the city and its liberties have eventually been battered to pieces. Book II opens at the start of the fourteenth century with the nobles in power. This led directly to the tyranny of the duke of Athens in 1342, when the citizens 'saw the majesty of their government ruined, her customs destroyed, her statutes annulled' (1128). They accordingly turned against the tyrant and succeeded in setting up their own popular regime. But, as Machiavelli goes on to relate in Book III, this in turn degenerated into licence when the 'unrestrained mob' managed to seize control of the republic in 1378 (1161–3). Next the pendulum swung back to 'the aristocrats of popular origin', and by the middle of the fifteenth century they were seeking once again to curtail the liberties of the people, thereby encouraging a new form of tyrannical government (1188).

It is true that, when Machiavelli arrives at this final phase of his narrative in Books VII and VIII, he begins to present his argument in a more oblique and cautious style. His central topic is inescapably the rise of the Medici, and he clearly feels that some allowance must be made for the fact that the same family had made it possible for him to write his *History*. While he takes considerable pains to dissemble his hostility, however, it is easy to recover his feelings about the Medicean contribution to Florentine history if we piece together certain sections of the argument which he is careful to keep separate.

Book VII opens with a general discussion of the most insidious means by which a leading citizen can hope to corrupt the populace in such a way as to promote divisive factions and acquire absolute power for himself. The issue had already been extensively treated in the *Discourses*, and Machiavelli largely contents himself with reiterating his earlier arguments. The greatest danger is said to be that of permitting the rich to employ their wealth to gain 'partisans who follow them for personal profit' instead of following the public interest. He adds that there are two principal methods by which this can be done. One is 'by doing favours to various citizens, defending them from the magistrates, assisting them with money and aiding them in getting undeserved offices'. The other is 'by pleasing the masses with games and public gifts', putting on costly displays of a kind calculated to win a spurious popularity and lull the people into forfeiting their liberties (337).

If we turn with this analysis in mind to the last two books of the *History*, it is not difficult to detect the tone of aversion underlying Machiavelli's effusive descriptions of successive Medicean governments. He begins with Cosimo, on whom he lavishes a fine encomium in chapter 5 of Book VII, praising him in particular for surpassing 'every other in his time' not merely 'in influence and wealth but also in liberality'. It shortly becomes clear, however, that what Machiavelli has in mind is that by the time of his death 'there was no citizen of any standing in the city to whom Cosimo had not lent a large sum of money' (1342). The sinister implications of such studied munificence have already been pointed out. Next, Machiavelli moves on to the brief career of Cosimo's son, Piero de' Medici. At first he is described as 'good and honourable', but we soon learn that his sense of honour prompted him to lay on a series of chivalric tournaments and other festivities that were so elaborate and splendid that the city was kept busy for months in preparing and presenting them (1352). As before, we have already been warned about the harmful influence of such blatant appeals to the masses. Finally, when Machiavelli comes to the years of Lorenzo the Magnificent – and thus to the period of his own youth – he scarcely troubles to suppress the rising note of antipathy. By this stage, he declares, 'the Fortune and the liberality' of the Medici had so decisively done their corrupting work that 'the people had been made deaf' to the very idea of throwing off the Medicean tyranny, in consequence of which 'Liberty was not known in Florence' any more (1393).

The Final Misfortune

Despite Florence's relapse into tyranny, despite the return of the barbarians, Machiavelli felt able to comfort himself with the reflection that Italy had been spared the worst degradation of all. Although the barbarians had conquered, they had not succeeded in putting to the sword any of Italy's greatest cities. As he observes in *The Art of War*, Tortona may have been sacked 'but not Milan, Capua but not Naples, Brescia but not Venice' and – finally and most symbolically of all – 'Ravenna but not Rome' (624).

Machiavelli ought to have known better than to tempt Fortune with such overconfident sentiments. For in May 1527 the unthinkable happened. During the previous year, Francis I had treacherously entered a League to recover the possessions in Italy which he had been forced to cede after his crushing defeat at the hands of the imperial forces in 1525. Responding to this renewed challenge, Charles V ordered his armies back into Italy in the spring of 1527. But the troops were unpaid and badly disciplined, and instead of attacking any military targets they advanced directly on Rome. Entering the undefended city on 6 May, they put it to the sack in a four-day massacre that astounded and horrified the entire Christian world.

With the fall of Rome, Clement VII had to flee for his life. And with the loss of papal backing, the increasingly unpopular government of the Medici in Florence immediately collapsed. On 16 May the city council met to proclaim the restoration of the republic, and on the following morning the young Medicean princes rode out of the city and into exile.

For Machiavelli, with his staunchly republican sympathies, the restoration of free government in Florence ought to have been a moment of triumph. But in view of his connections with the Medici, who had been paying his salary for the past six years, he must have appeared to the younger generation of republicans as little more than an ageing and insignificant client of the discredited tyranny. Although he seems to have nurtured some hopes of regaining his old position in the second chancery, there was no question of any job being found for him in the new anti-Medicean government.

The irony of it all seems to have broken Machiavelli's spirit, and soon afterwards he contracted an illness from which he never recovered. The story that he summoned a priest to his deathbed to hear a final confession is one that most biographers have repeated, but it is undoubtedly a pious invention of a later date. Machiavelli had viewed the Church's ministrations with disdain throughout his life, and there is no evidence that he changed his mind at the moment of death. He died on 21 June, in the midst of his family and friends, and was buried in the church of Santa Croce on the following day.

With Machiavelli, more than with any other political theorist, the temptation to pursue him beyond the grave, to end by summarizing and sitting in judgement on his philosophy, is one that has generally proved irresistible. The process began immediately after his death, and it continues to this day. Some of Machiavelli's earliest critics, such as Francis Bacon, felt able to concede that 'we are much beholden to Machiavel and others, that write what men do, and not what they ought to do'. But the majority of Machiavelli's original readers were so shocked by his outlook that they simply denounced him as an invention of the devil, or even as Old Nick, the devil himself. By contrast, the bulk of Machiavelli's modern commentators have confronted even his most outrageous doctrines with an air of conscious worldliness. But some of them, especially Leo Strauss and his disciples, have unrepentantly continued to uphold the traditional view that (as Strauss expresses it) Machiavelli can only be characterized as 'a teacher of evil'.

The business of the historian, however, is surely to serve as a recording angel, not a hanging judge. All I have accordingly sought to do in the preceding pages is to recover the past and place it before the present, without trying to employ the local and defeasible standards of the present as a way of praising or blaming the past. As the inscription on Machiavelli's tomb proudly reminds us, 'no epitaph can match so great a name'.

Works by Machiavelli Quoted in the Text

The Art of War, in *Machiavelli: The Chief Works and Others*, trans. A. Gilbert, 3 vols (Durham, NC, 1965), 561–726.

Caprices [*Ghiribizzi*], in R. Ridolfi and P. Ghiglieri, 'I Ghiribizzi al Soderini', *La Bibliofilia*, 72 (1970), 71–4.

Correspondence [*Lettere*], ed. F. Gaeta (Milan, 1961).

Discourses on the first Decade of Titus Livius, in *Machiavelli*, trans. Gilbert, 175–529.

The History of Florence, in *Machiavelli*, trans. Gilbert, 1025–1435.

The Legations [*Legazioni e commissarie*], ed. S. Bertelli, 3 vols (Milan, 1964).

The Life of Castruccio Castracani of Lucca, in *Machiavelli*, trans. Gilbert, 533–59.

The Prince, ed. Q. Skinner and R. Price (Cambridge, 1988).

A Provision for Infantry, in *Machiavelli*, trans. Gilbert, 3.

Further Reading

Bibliography

Silvia Ruffo Fiore, *Niccolò Machiavelli: An Annotated Bibliography of Modern Criticism and Scholarship* (New York, 1990) covers the previous half-century of studies. For an analysis of my own approach see Roberta Talamo, 'Quentin Skinner interprete di Machiavelli', *Croce Via* 3 (1997), pp. 80–101.

Biography

The standard work remains Roberto Ridolfi, *The Life of Niccolò Machiavelli*, trans. Cecil Grayson (1963). Sebastian de Grazia, *Machiavelli in Hell* (Princeton, 1989) is an unusual intellectual biography. John M. Najemy, *Between Friends: Discourses of Power and Desire in the Machiavelli-Vettori Letters of 1513–1515* (Princeton, 1993) concentrates on the period in which *The Prince* was written. For the most up-to-date account see Maurizio Viroli, *Il sorriso de Niccolò: Storia di Machiavelli* (Rome, 1998).

The Political Context

For the period of Machiavelli's youth see Nicolai Rubinstein, *The Government of Florence under the Medici 1434–1494* (Oxford, 1966). On the 1490s see Donald Weinstein, *Savonarola and Florence* (Princeton, 1963). On Machiavelli's political and diplomatic career see the section 'Machiavelli and the Republican Experience' – essays by Nicolai

Rubinstein, Elena Fasano Guarini, Giovanni Silvano, Robert Black, and John M. Najemy – in *Machiavelli and Republicanism*, ed. Gisela Bock, Quentin Skinner, and Maurizio Viroli (Cambridge, 1990), pp. 1–117. On the vicissitudes of the Florentine republic during Machiavelli's adult life see Rudolf von Albertini, *Firenze dalla repubblica al principato* (Turin, 1970), H. C. Butters, *Governors and Government in Early Sixteenth-Century Florence, 1502–1519* (Oxford, 1985), and J. N. Stephens, *The Fall of the Florentine Republic, 1512–1530* (Oxford, 1983).

The Intellectual Context

The essays collected in P. O. Kristeller, *Renaissance Thought*, 2 vols (New York, 1961–65) remain indispensable. For the fullest survey of the intellectual life of the period see *The Cambridge History of Renaissance Philosophy*, ed. Charles Schmitt, Eckhard Kessler, Quentin Skinner, and Jill Kraye (Cambridge, 1988). For the classic account of 'civic humanism' see Hans Baron, *The Crisis of the Early Italian Renaissance* (revised edn, Princeton, 1966). See also Donald J. Wilcox, *The Development of Florentine Humanist Historiography in the Fifteenth Century* (Cambridge, Mass., 1969) and Peter Godman, *From Poliziano to Machiavelli: Florentine Humanism in the High Renaissance* (Princeton, 1998). For surveys of the political theory of the period see Quentin Skinner, *The Foundations of Modern Political Thought*, 2 vols (Cambridge, 1978) and *The Cambridge History of Political Thought 1450–1700*, ed. J. H. Burns and Mark Goldie (Cambridge, 1991).

General Studies of Machiavelli's Political Thought

The fullest outline is Gennaro Sasso, *Niccolò Machiavelli I. Il pensiero politico* (Bologna, 1980). A classic work is Felix Gilbert, *Machiavelli and Guicciardini: Politics and History in Sixteenth-Century Italy* (revised edn, New York, 1984). Mark Hulliung, *Citizen Machiavelli* (Princeton, 1983) stresses Machiavelli's subversion of classical humanism. Leo Strauss, *Thoughts on Machiavelli* (Glencoe, Ill., 1958) views him as 'a teacher of evil'. The place of religion in Machiavelli's thought has been valuably reappraised in a symposium – with contributions by John H. Geerken,

Marcia L. Colish, Cary J. Nederman, Benedetto Fontana, and John M. Najemy – in the *Journal of the History of Ideas* 60 (1999), pp. 579–681. See also Anthony J. Parel, *The Machiavellian Cosmos* (New Haven, 1992).

Machiavelli's Political Vocabulary

J. H. Whitfield, 'On Machiavelli's Use of *Ordini*' in *Discourses on Machiavelli* (Cambridge, 1969), pp. 141–62. J. H. Hexter, '*Il Principe* and *lo stato*' in *The Vision of Politics on the Eve of the Reformation* (London, 1973), pp. 150–78. Russell Price, 'The Senses of *Virtú* in Machiavelli' in *European Studies Review* 4 (1973), pp. 315–45. Russell Price, 'The Theme of *Gloria* in Machiavelli' in *Renaissance Quarterly* 30 (1977), pp. 588–631. Victor A. Santi, *La 'Gloria' nel pensiero di Machiavelli* (Ravenna, 1979). Quentin Skinner, 'Machiavelli on the Maintenance of Liberty' in *Politics*, 18 (1983), pp. 3–15. Hanna Fenichel Pitkin, *Fortune is a Woman: Gender and Politics in the Thought of Niccolò Machiavelli* (Berkeley, Cal., 1984). Russell Price, 'Self-Love, "Egoism" and *Ambizione* in Machiavelli's Thought' in *History of Political Thought* 9 (1988), pp. 237–61. Harvey C. Mansfield, *Machiavelli's Virtue* (Chicago, 1996).

Machiavelli's Rhetoric

This has recently become a major focus of research. For pioneering studies see Nancy S. Struever, *The Language of History in the Renaissance: Rhetoric and Historical Consciousness in Florentine Humanism* (Princeton, 1970) and Brian Richardson, 'Notes on Machiavelli's Sources and his Treatment of the Rhetorical Tradition', *Italian Studies* 26 (1971), pp. 24–48. The first part of Victoria Kahn, *Machiavellian Rhetoric from the Counter-Reformation to Milton* (Princeton, 1994) considers the rhetoric of Machiavelli's *Prince* and *Discourses*. Quentin Skinner, 'Thomas Hobbes: Rhetoric and the Construction of Morality' in *Proceedings of the British Academy* 76, pp. 1–61, highlights Machiavelli's use of rhetorical redescription. Virginia Cox, 'Machiavelli and the *Rhetorica ad Herennium*: Deliberative Rhetoric in *The Prince*' in *Sixteenth Century Journal* 28 (1997) connects Machiavelli's vocabulary directly to the Roman *ars rhetorica*.

Maurizio Viroli, *Machiavelli* (Oxford, 1998) lays particular emphasis on the rhetorical character of Machiavelli's thought.

Studies of *The Prince*
Hans Baron, 'Machiavelli: The Republican Citizen and the Author of *The Prince*' in *The English Historical Review* 76 (1961), pp. 217–53. Felix Gilbert, 'The Humanist Concept of the Prince and *The Prince* of Machiavelli' in *History: Choice and Commitment* (Cambridge, Mass., 1977), pp. 91–114. Marcia Colish, 'Cicero's *De Officiis* and Machiavelli's *Prince*' in *Sixteenth Century Journal* 9 (1978), pp. 81–94. J. Jackson Barlow, 'The Fox and the Lion: Machiavelli Replies to Cicero' in *History of Political Thought* 20 (1999), pp. 627–45.

Studies of the *Discourses*
For a classic reading of the text and its context see J. G. A. Pocock, *The Machiavellian Moment: Florentine Political Thought and the Atlantic Republican Tradition* (Princeton, 1975), Part II, 'The Republic and its Fortune', pp. 81–330. On the broader setting of Machiavelli's republicanism see Maurizio Viroli, *From Politics to Reason of State: The Acquisition and Transformation of the Language of Politics, 1250–1600* (Cambridge, 1992). Harvey Mansfield, *Machiavelli's New Modes and Orders* (Ithaca, 1979) offers a chapter-by-chapter commentary. More specialized studies include Felix Gilbert, 'The Composition and Structure of Machiavelli's *Discorsi*' in *History: Choice and Commitment*, 1977, pp. 115–33; Felix Gilbert, 'Bernardo Rucellai and the Orti Oricellari: A Study on the Origin of Modern Political Thought' in *History: Choice and Commitment*, 1977, pp. 215–46; Quentin Skinner, 'Machiavelli's *Discorsi* and the Pre-humanist Origins of Republican Ideas' in *Machiavelli and Republicanism*, ed. Bock, Skinner, and Viroli, pp. 121–41.

Studies of *The History of Florence*
The fullest analysis is Gennaro Sasso, *Niccolò Machiavelli II. La storiografia* (Bologna, 1993). The following detailed studies are of particular importance: Felix Gilbert, 'Machiavelli's *Istorie Fiorentine*: An Essay in

Interpretation' in *History: Choice and Commitment*, 1977, pp. 135–53; John M. Najemy '*Arti* and *Ordini* in Machiavelli's *Istorie Fiorentine*' in *Essays Presented to Myron P. Gilmore* ed. Sergio Bertelli and Gloria Ramakus, 2 vols (Florence, 1978), pp. 161–91; Carlo Dionisotti, 'Machiavelli storico' in *Machiavellerie* (Turin, 1980), pp. 365–409 and Gisela Bock, 'Civil Discord in Machiavelli's *Istorie Fiorentine*' in *Machiavelli and Republicanism*, ed. Bock, Skinner and Viroli 1990, pp. 181–201.

Index

Index

Expand your collection of
VERY SHORT INTRODUCTIONS

Visit the
VERY SHORT INTRODUCTIONS
Web site

www.oup.co.uk/vsi

➤ **Information** about all published titles

➤ News of **forthcoming books**

➤ **Extracts** from the books, including titles not yet published

➤ **Reviews** and views

➤ **Links** to other **web sites** and main OUP web page

➤ Information about **VSIs in translation**

➤ **Contact** the editors

➤ **Order** other **VSIs** on-line